For Gene,
with best wishes—
Don.

The Comic Theatre

The Comic Theatre

A Comedy in Three Acts by
CARLO GOLDONI

Translated from the Italian by
JOHN W. MILLER

With an Introduction by
DONALD CHENEY

UNIVERSITY OF NEBRASKA PRESS · LINCOLN

Publishers on the Plains

UNP

Manufactured in the United States of America

Contents

Introduction

The Comic Theatre hovers uneasily between the realms of drama and literary criticism. Although it was originally written for the theatre, and seems to have found favor on its first performance in 1750 (at a time when the appetite for Carlo Goldoni's plays was apparently insatiable), it has rarely been performed subsequently, and then only as an act of homage to its author's genius, for example in connection with academic celebrations of Goldonian anniversaries. Both as a play and as an expression of literary theory, in fact, it must be seen in terms of its "festive" elements: its plot emphasizes the fundamental harmony of all the characters, to the virtual suppression of any serious challenge from the old-fashioned viewpoints of Lelio or Eleonora, who are only too eager to be invited to Orazio's luncheon; and the critical theory enunciated in the play is less a critical manifesto than the celebration of a theatrical reform already accomplished and recognized.

Considered as a play, the work doubtless suffers from its lack of suspense, as Goldoni himself implies in his prefatory epistle to the reader: it is "less a comedy in itself than a Foreword to all my Comedies." But even as a theoretical statement of the principles of Goldonian comedy, it calls for some further prefatory remarks before a modern reader can understand its basic assumptions. The difficulty seems to come from two related but distinct problems. In the first place, as a triumphant testimony to Goldoni's reform of the stage, it shares with other victory celebrations elements of smugness and complacency, of response to an audience's demand for mutual congratulation ("Just think of the greater fame actors have now"; "Our Italians demand much more [than French audiences]"; "But to compose comedies in such a way is extremely difficult"), with little evidence of any redeeming modesty or self-awareness. But beyond this blandness of style in the play itself, one is troubled by a more serious sense of complacent optimism in the very theory of comedy asserted by Goldoni.

A modern reader cannot approach *The Comic Theatre*, with its repeated parallelism of the real and fictional identities of the actors preparing their play within the play, without recalling how similar dramatic situations led to profound questionings of art and the reality it pretends to reflect, both in Pirandello and in those Elizabethan dramatists whom Goldoni admired. Orazio's instructions to Eleonora (III.iii) seem to echo Hamlet's similar instructions to his players, but in an infinitely narrower context. Doubtless such an echo is unfair to Goldoni, or to any comic author for that matter; but it may serve to introduce some of the genuine concerns of Goldoni's theatre as they are enunciated in this play. Goldoni has chosen as his spokesman an impresario whose name, Orazio, recalls those Horatian ideals of balance and moderation in all things which Hamlet found in his Horatio; and the emphasis on craftsmanship and common sense, together with the numerous Latin tags scattered through the play, similarly recalls the tone of Horace's *Poetics*, as Orazio's commentary on that work makes clear when he corrects the overly rigorous interpretation by Lelio (III.ix). A fuller understanding of Goldoni's conception of his position in relation to the theatre of his time may serve first to give relevance to his literary theory, and secondly to suggest how a play so lacking in dramatic suspense as *The Comic Theatre* could have proved interesting to its Venetian audience in 1750. To understand the dramatic economy of the play, finally, is to see how it embodies Goldoni's sense of the prospects open to Italian comedy.

In contrast to the theatres of other countries—England and more recently France and Spain—native Italian dramatic productions tended to be relatively undeveloped by the early eighteenth century. The opera had risen to prominence, as the new houses in Verona and Naples testified; and there remained a tradition of learned, aristocratic drama in the Italian courts. But for Goldoni in Venice especially, the dominant theatrical tradition remained that of the legitimate stage, or "theatre of professionals" (the literal meaning of *commedia dell' arte*), presided over by companies of actors who relied less on the novelty of individual plays than on their own ability to extemporize comic business in connection with a limited number of stock situations. The actors of the *commedia dell' arte*, literally as well as figuratively confined by the masks of a handful of such familiar characters as Harlequin or Colombina, worked from a "scenario," or outline of scenes, which made minimal demands on the talents of a playwright. Novelty was provided by the ability of the individual actor to work variations on his traditional role. With the aid of promptbooks or *generici* containing the commonplaces appropriate to a given situation, he could spin out an extended improvisation to swell a scene and demonstrate his own skill. The inevitable drift of the *commedia dell' arte* was therefore toward a burlesque or music hall entertainment in which the comic plot was taken for granted and the interest of the audience directed toward the individual performances of its favorite comedians. The comedians, in turn, were driven by the poverty of their roles to ever increasing grossness of gesture and dialogue in their search for novelty and variation.

It seems likely that actors and audience alike had become aware that in this genre of *commedia dell' arte* the Italian theatre had reached a dead end, for the ease with which Goldoni was able to find an appreciative forum for his earliest efforts and to introduce his proposed reforms suggests that he faced no problem of an entrenched guild of actors clinging jealously to their traditional autonomy. Probably Tonino in *The Comic Theatre* speaks for the majority of his colleagues in lamenting the complexity of the new theatre while conceding that it is vastly more popular and hence more profitable than the old. In his return to "premeditated" comedies in which a playwright's overriding sense of character and plot line gave shape to the individual speeches, Goldoni was able to respond to an awareness of social realities which had become blunted in the older burlesque.

Goldoni's plays, it should be noted, pose a striking challenge to modern directors, especially in translation. The present version of *The Comic Theatre* has sought to provide a coherent and lucid translation, remaining close to the literal meaning for the benefit of students; it has made few of those many adaptations toward modern equivalents of eighteenth-century stylistic distinctions which a modern production would want to attempt. It should be remembered, in the first place, that the traditional *commedia dell' arte* distinguished the masked comic figures—the Venetian Pantalone, the Bolognese Doctor, the Bergamese zanies Harlequin and Brighella —from the unmasked pairs of lovers who spoke in Italian and were thus closer to the audience's sentimental norm, rather in the manner of their descendants in the modern musical comedy. Under the democratizing force of Goldoni's reform, however, this crude distinction becomes infinitely complicated. Masked buffoon and unmasked lover alike are given written parts which show them alternating between their real selves and the charades they enact in their social roles. It is a central premise of Goldoni's view of comedy that light should be cast upon those members of the company who feel themselves most secure in their dignity: the musician or the poet, who are revealed as starving comedians whose pretensions seem hilarious to the professional, avowed buffoons among the players. A study of the techniques of the *commedia dell' arte*[1] will emphasize the first and most obvious contrast of styles, that between the masked and the more respectable characters; but upon that contrast and in counterpoint to it, the discerning producer will build the slighter exaggerations of gesture which characterize Lelio and Eleonora on

[1] Students interested in pursuing the history of the *commedia dell' arte* may begin with Allardyce Nicoll, *The World of Harlequin: A Critical Study of the Commedia dell' arte* (Cambridge, 1963). Nicoll provides a useful bibliography of writings since 1930 (some of them in English), as well as many illustrations of costumes adopted by Harlequin and his companions through the centuries. He further offers bibliographic and visual detail on other aspects of the subject in two books, *Masks, Mimes and Miracles: Studies in the Popular Theatre* (1931; reprinted New York, 1963) and *The Development of the Theatre* (London, 1927). Another illustrated volume is by P. L. Duchartre, *The Italian Comedy*, trans. R. T. Weaver (London, 1929). K. M. Lea, *Italian Popular Comedy* (2 vols.; 1934; reprinted New York, 1962), emphasizes English connections with the *commedia*.

their first appearance. Any attempt to stage this play would be conditioned by the special interests and background of the audience. A playwright like Goldoni, whose wit is so closely linked to a specific time and place, must be translated freely if he is to survive on stage. For such a dramatic translation the present text, ironically, may seem little more than a scenario, a set of notes from which the professional actors must draw inspiration for their own acts of improvisation.

In his repeated emphasis on the realism of his theatre, Goldoni relies on his audience's awareness of a gap between theatre and life in the *commedia dell' arte*. His reformed theatre, he would argue, gives a newly found relevance to the stage. The bourgeois Venetian audience can see its own world reflected directly in his comedies. Neither aristocratic spectacle nor plebeian farce, his social comedies present recognizable middle-class values, marked with a distinctly local accent that contemporary translations from the French stage could not provide. It is in this sense that Orazio's troupe rejoices that obscenities have been banished from the stage, not only in the interest of family entertainment— "Now young ladies can go to the theatre without fear of learning anything immodest or insidious" (III.iii)—but also on the basis of reflecting actual social practice (I.xi). By reflecting the norms of accepted polite behavior, the comedians show us the real world of the audience (or at least what that audience likes to consider real), and at the same time, they contribute to its moral development. Orazio concedes (II.iii) that sinful (though not scandalous) characters may be presented on stage, but only in secondary roles where they may be the more easily overcome by examples of virtue.

Such an emphasis on the continuing triumph of virtue throughout the action of a comedy may well constitute a serious handicap to Goldoni's creation of the obstructionist figures essential to comedy—those jealous husbands or parents who stand in the way of lovers and create situations which challenge the happy society. Orazio's criteria would leave little room for the creation of a Tartuffe, for instance; and even the more ordinary difficulties of young lovers tend to be understated in Goldoni's works—as is the case with the farce in *The Comic Theatre* where Pantalone's threat is quickly overcome, in almost perfunctory fashion. But for Goldoni this diminution in plot suspense is a small price to pay for the advantages of having a cast of fundamentally good-natured characters who can be easily recognized by the audience, whom they resemble. By reacting in this way against the earlier grossness of characterization, the reformed theatre can now be understood and evaluated by all its spectators:

> And let me tell you why. Comedy was created to correct vice and ridicule bad customs; when the ancient poets wrote comedies in this manner, the common people could participate because, seeing the copy of a character on stage, each found the original either in himself or in someone else. But when comedies became merely ridiculous, no one paid attention any more, because with the excuse of making people laugh, they admitted the worst and the most blatant errors. But now that we have returned to fish comedies from nature's *Mare Magnum*, men feel their hearts touched again. They can identify with the characters or passions and discern whether a character is well observed and developed, and whether a passion is well motivated. (II.i)

With their appeal to a social realism based on the moral usefulness of drama, Anselmo's words help to explain the attractiveness of Goldoni's plays to modern Russian audiences. And they attempt as well to justify a successful author's willingness to be judged on the basis of his popularity. Now that Italian audiences have been given a comic theatre which reflects their interests, they have become the best judges of theatrical effectiveness. Repeatedly it is their applause—or its consequences for Orazio's cash box—which provides the court of last appeal against traditional practices and honored critical assumptions.

Goldoni's projection of himself as a working playwright, a craftsman who seeks above all to earn an honest living and stand aloof from critical bickering, is more immediately evident in his defense of *The Cunning Widow*, written under the pressure of Pietro Chiari's satirical assault in 1749. Here Goldoni is arguing specific technical problems of dramatic plausibility; the basic concept of a reformed stage has been accepted. Chiari shares Goldoni's premises: indeed, both playwrights will be condemned as sentimentalists by their contemporary, the Venetian Carlo Gozzi, whose aristocratic nostalgia for the fantastic world of traditional *commedia dell' arte* is opposed to any intrusion of bourgeois realism. Within this newly reformed theatre, however, Goldoni quickly discovers that his insistence on naturalism can lead to innumerable disputes over the plausibility of individual incidents, disguises, foreign accents, and the like. To all such disputes his instinctive response is to retreat from critical theory to consider the immediate results of his practices: "I appeal to the audience. Let them judge, and I will submit to them." Rather than embroil himself in "criticism" (a term which means "libel" or "satire" in Goldoni's usage), he appeals for good temper between playwrights and dramatic characters as well. He begins his defense by dissociating himself from Chiari's efforts to draw undiscriminating laughter at the expense of foreigners or through a "fool who disguises herself pointlessly." He goes on to question

Chiari's patriotism in ridiculing a fellow Italian on the stage; and he concludes by seeing Chiari's attack on himself as a part of this cheap and graceless buffoonery: "I am not one to ridicule people on stage, even if I had good reason to do it. . . . When playwrights and players speak ill of each other, and use the theatre as a forum for slander, they reach the level of charlatans."

The arguments produced in heat under Chiari's attack are reflected more temperately in *The Comic Theatre*. Lelio's final assertion (III.ix), that criticism is the "one thing that will always be appreciated in the theatre," draws Orazio's concluding remark that such criticism must always be "moderate," must aim "at the universal, not the particular": it must never be permitted to fall into satire. In moving away from any satirical thrust in his comedies, Goldoni tends to cast his "comedies of character" in benevolent terms. Though he may continue to speak of correcting vices and defects through ridicule, in practice his characters show defects which are so modest as to verge on triviality, and a spirit of good-natured festivity prevails. The sixteen plays which Goldoni composed for the single season of 1750/1751 testify not only to his extraordinary energy but to his ability to embrace a broad range of farcical and sentimental themes. As a prologue to that season's offerings, *The Comic Theatre* is itself an example of the playwright's concern for reconciling divergent dramatic principles. There is a hint of reconciliation at the end of the Apologetic Prologue; this theme becomes paramount in the later work.

If the premise of Goldoni's reform was the reassertion of the playwright's authority over the troupe of players, it may be significant of such a spirit of reconciliation that Goldoni's spokesman in *The Comic Theatre* is the leader of the actors, Girolamo Medebach, who had functioned more passively as Prudenzio in the Apologetic Prologue. As the man responsible for the financial and artistic success of the company, Orazio is from the outset preoccupied with questions of economy. In the first scene of the play, the very fact that we are permitted an informal glimpse of the players is owing to his decision that the cost of lamps outweighs the dangers of any loss of novelty. And it is in terms of such thrift that the morning's rehearsal is developed. Orazio must placate the first arrivals lest they leave before the others come; from his conversation it emerges that they must begin their season with a farce while waiting for the two additional parts needed to perform the full-scale comedies of character. Throughout the opening scenes, Orazio goes about his task of good-natured diplomacy, making the most of the dramatic means at his disposal. Placida, who is the first to speak on behalf of the new style, reluctantly consents to perform in an old-fashioned comedy, since under Orazio's guidance she knows that "at least the actors will be properly directed and the sentiments will be well handled." But she warns that the new actors must be found soon or she will leave the company.

The initial plot line, therefore, might be seen as the quest for a complete company of actors. In practice this theme is scarcely presented with any degree of urgency; yet it does give point to the two new arrivals, Lelio and Eleonora. At heart both of them are unemployed actors, with pretensions to supposedly higher roles in the theatre. Lelio presents himself as a poet, but is forced to admit that in the new theatre actors and audience alike are better informed than he. Eleonora presents herself as a musical virtuoso set apart from "mere" actors, but she comes to accept gratefully her role as an equal of the other players. In both cases the new arrivals are already driven by hunger; the public has already passed judgment on their old-fashioned styles and their discordant claims for individual attention at the expense of the play itself. If the players need them to complete the cast, they need employment with equal urgency. To the extent that they present any challenge to the play's happy conclusion, therefore, they serve as spokesmen for earlier prejudices, to be educated by Orazio's teachings and by his company's good example.

In terms of the forging of the company's unity, the other characters function similarly in the opening scenes: their various points of view suggest the synthesis represented by Orazio's concept of comedy. Placida disdains the old *commedia dell' arte* but is persuaded to accept it; she is followed (I.iv) by Tonino, who comes on in the character of Pantalone, doing comic turns in Venetian accent while lamenting the difficulties of the new style. Orazio placates him as well, and coaxes a song out of him with the audience's assistance.

Vittoria, who arrives next, is shown as a diligent student of her role, in contrast to the two complaining players who have preceded her. Orazio banters with her on the subject of her role as gold digger, but beneath the debate between the sexes the point is emphasized that in reality actresses are no different from other women. Here and in the following scene the audience is assured that "an actor must be honorable like everyone else; he must know his duty, love honor and all the moral virtues."

By such devices Goldoni is advancing his claim to be presenting a reflection of the bourgeois moral reality of his audience. But Orazio's company is too varied in its makeup for these moral overtones to dominate. No sooner does one character assert the distinction between public and private roles, than another comes on wholly absorbed in his masquerade. Gianni, like Tonino before him, is one of the dialect characters in his first appearance (I.viii): his comic turn leads Orazio to wonder whether he is acting as Harlequin or speaking in his native accents. And Gianni's comments on the question of how he should speak raise playfully the questions of decorum and realism that Chiari had broached earlier in his attack on *The Cunning Widow*. The only sound determination of the dialect appropriate to Harlequins must be based on a scientific survey of how they really speak. Or alternatively, Gianni suggests, a Bergamese becomes rebaptized a Venetian when he falls into the Grand Canal. The burden of all these quibbles is that a clown refuses to abide by strict rules of clownish decorum. Orazio is tolerantly approving of such freedom: "In a Harlequin even verses are bearable."

These scenes prior to Lelio's arrival provide varied elements of entertainment: they suggest the range of Orazio's company and the mixture of theatrical conventions which these players embody. Orazio's role as their good-natured but hard-pressed leader establishes his credentials as a spokesman once Lelio presents himself. Above all, we have been shown a harmonious company working together and relieving the strain of rehearsal by playful alternation between their private and public personalities. Lelio is set apart from the others at first by the humorless ceremony of his behavior. Where Orazio has brought all the actors together by his ability to speak to each on his own terms, Lelio quickly undoes his work as he begins to recite his play. One by one the actors cap his lines with rhyming insults and make their exit (in the old-fashioned manner, as we were reminded at the beginning of Act I, scene vii), until Lelio is left alone on stage, vowing revenge. The first act concludes with the disintegration of the Comic Theatre under the influence of the false poet.

The opening lines of Act II make abundantly clear, however, that Lelio has no intention of taking his play elsewhere as he has threatened. He confesses his desperation to Anselmo, who replies knowledgeably, though in the dialect of his role as Brighella, with the result that Lelio admits to himself that these comedians know more than he does. In succeeding scenes, however, he continues to maintain his affectations, with the result that it is not until Act II, scene xii, that he is brought to confess his destitution to Orazio and is admitted to the company of players, just before Eleonora arrives to undergo a similar initiation. In the meantime, however, he has begun to make friends with the other players, so that his acceptance by Orazio is a consequence of his being befriended by Anselmo. By the third act, indeed, his role is no longer wholly that of foil to Orazio's superior understanding. In Act III, scene ii, he steps quite out of character to recite lines of verse which are unknown to Orazio but which prove to have been written by "the author of your plays."

It is doubtless a token of Lelio's assimilation into the troupe that he can now jest lightly and ironically in the manner of the other players. But there is a special point to this irony in Lelio's case. Lelio hints at a private relationship to the author: of the verses he says, "Actually he didn't want to write them, but to me, a fellow poet, he has confided this scene."

ORAZIO: Then you know him?
LELIO: Yes, I know him and hope some day to be able to compose comedies as he does.

Goldoni seems to be flirting here with an identification between himself and Lelio, the false poet who is nevertheless the only poet shown on stage. And again, in the concluding lines of the play, Lelio interrupts the rehearsal for the last time to assert triumphantly that his own play ends in the same way. Indeed, Lelio's title, *A Father His Daughters' Pander*, which Orazio had earlier criticized for its scandalous overtones, is from one point of view merely the complement to that of the play within the play, *A Father His Son's Rival*. Lelio had earlier proposed (I.xi) that a play might be presented annually under the name of a separate character, and something of this sort might apply here if the farce were seen to focus equally on the two fathers involved. At any rate, the distance between the two poets, Lelio and Goldoni, has narrowed to the point that Orazio is content to yield his new player the pleasures of identification with the master, as regards both the conclusion of the farce and the possibility of a concluding sonnet as well. The hour is late and the players are eager to leave.

The Comic Theatre does not insist on such an identification between Lelio and Goldoni, to be sure. But its symmetries and parallelisms of structure are so extensive as to suggest Goldoni's awareness that his strength as a playwright lay in the assimilation of the resources of the native Italian tradition to his own bourgeois idealism. The fact that Orazio and his enlightened company are nevertheless limited to the enactment of farces until they accept and assimilate these two foolish "outsiders," together with the play's movement toward the simultaneous conclusions of the farce and the demonstration of "what, in our judgment, ought to be our Comic Theatre," implies that the healthy playwright, like the healthy society, must accept all of its discordant elements. Orazio may be pained by the cost of his luncheon (and the coffee hour at the end of Act III), but these are the prices he must pay. Subsequent generations of critics have often remarked that Goldoni's strength lay in the very elements of *commedia dell' arte* against which his reform seemed to be directed; *The Comic Theatre* suggests his own awareness of this fact.

DONALD CHENEY

University of Massachusetts

Translator's Note

As Goldoni indicates in his prefatory letter, *The Comic Theatre* was first published in 1751 in Venice, in Volume II of Bettinelli's edition of the plays. This translation is based on the standard modern edition, that of Giuseppe Ortolani (Volume II, Mondadori, Verona, 1936), which in turn follows the definitive text—corrected by Goldoni himself—of Pasquali (Volume I, Venice, 1761). Another edition authorized by Goldoni was that of Zatta (44 volumes, 1788–1795). Footnotes which are printed in this translation in italics appear in the earliest editions of the play and are presumably Goldoni's.

I should like to express my gratitude to Eric Bentley, who first suggested this translation and helped in numerous ways to see it into print.

J. W. M.

New York

The Comic Theatre

The Author to the Reader[1]

This work which I entitle *The Comic Theatre* should be called less a Comedy in itself than a Foreword to all my Comedies. In the Edition I had begun in Venice it appeared in the Second Tome, being written after the First Tome had been printed. Even by then, however, as I had written in my letter to the Publisher sent from Turin in 1751, I had expressed my desire to have it placed, if possible, at the head of all my works, to serve, as I have mentioned, as a Foreword. Now that I have the opportunity to do so, I am more satisfied.

Whatever name one may give to this composition, I have tried here to state explicitly a large part of those defects which I myself have attempted to avoid, and all the principles on which I have based my own method for writing Comedies; and no other difference exists between this piece and a more conventional introduction, except that the latter would probably have bored readers more easily, while in this I have partially avoided this tedium with the help of some action.

It is not my intention to provide new rules for others, but only to let it be known that, with long observation and nearly continuous practice, I have reached the point where

---

[1] This prefatory note by Goldoni was first included in Volume I of Paperini's edition (Florence, 1753).

I could open a road for myself on which I could walk with some greater certitude; and this finds no little proof in the enjoyment that the Spectators receive from my Comedies. I should hope that anyone who devotes himself to writing, no matter in what field, would inform others about the road he has chosen to follow, since it would always serve as a means for illuminating and improving the arts.

And likewise, I strongly desire that some brilliant Italian mind would undertake to perfect my own work, and thereby return lost honor to our stage with fine Comedies: true Comedies, that is, and not scenes slapped together with neither order nor rule; and I, who to this day may have appeared to some as wanting to act the role of the Teacher, will never feel ashamed to learn something from someone who has the ability to instruct.

I had this play produced in 1750 the first night of the Autumn Season as the opening work of the Theatre. At that time this work included those homages which Actors usually pay to the Audience, but I later removed such sections as I deemed them of no use to the Comedy itself.

Furthermore, to conform to custom and to put the Company, and particularly the masked characters, in good favor, I introduced them first in their ordinary, everyday clothes and their own faces, and afterwards in costumes and stage masks. Later on, however, I felt that this was somewhat artificial, and now, in the present edition of this Comedy, I have also assigned a proper name to each Character, calling him by his stage name whenever he or she appears in a specific role in the rehearsal within the play. This is a further modification which occurred to me only now and will therefore constitute one more defect in the imperfect Bettinelli edition.

Characters

ORAZIO, *the head of the company of comic actors, called Ottavio in the rehearsal of the play within the play*

PLACIDA, *the leading lady, called Rosaura in the rehearsal*

BEATRICE, *the second lady*

EUGENIO, *the second* amoroso, *called Florindo in the rehearsal*

LELIO, *a poet*

ELEONORA, *a singer*

VITTORIA, *a theatre maid, called Colombina in the rehearsal*

TONINO,* *a Venetian, later Pantalone in the rehearsal*

PETRONIO, *who plays the Doctor in the rehearsal*

ANSELMO,* *who plays Brighella in the rehearsal*

GIANNI,* *who plays Harlequin in the rehearsal*

THE PROMPTER

A FOOTMAN *of the singer, who speaks*

THEATRE SERVANTS, *who do not speak*

* These characters speak in Venetian dialect mixed with some touches of Lombard.

The scene, which remains unchanged throughout, is the comic stage itself, with flats and view of a room.[2] *Since it is daytime, there are neither lights nor spectators.*

[2] "Room": In Zatta's edition (1788–1795), "courtyard." The frontispiece is ambiguous in this respect, but in any case it is an interior setting which is described.

Act One

Scene I

The curtain rises and before it is entirely up, ORAZIO *steps forward, then* EUGENIO.

ORAZIO: *(Toward the stage.)* Stop, stop, don't raise the curtain, stop.

EUGENIO: Why not, Signor Orazio? Don't you want the curtain up, sir?

ORAZIO: When we're rehearsing the third act of a comedy there's no need to raise the curtain.

EUGENIO: Nor do we need to keep it lowered either.

ORAZIO: Ah, but there's a very good reason to keep it lowered, yes indeed, my dear Eugenio. You people don't understand what I have in mind. *(Toward the stage.)* Drop that curtain.

EUGENIO: *(Toward the stage.)* No, hold it there! If we drop the curtain we won't be able to see, and then, my dear director, in order to rehearse we will have to light the lamps.

ORAZIO: Well, in that case we'd better raise the curtain. *(Toward the stage.)* Hoist it up. I don't want to spend money on lamps.

EUGENIO: Bravo! Hurrah for thrift!

ORAZIO: My good friend, if I hadn't a little thrift, we'd be in a fine predicament. Actors never get rich; they spend whatever they earn. If they're lucky, they come out even at the end of the year, but for most of them what goes out is more than what comes in.

EUGENIO: Now would you kindly explain why you wanted to keep the curtain down?

ORAZIO: So no one could see us rehearsing our scenes.

EUGENIO: But who would ever come to the theatre in the middle of the morning?

ORAZIO: Oh, some curious souls would even rise before daybreak.

EUGENIO: But they've seen our company before. There can't be much curiosity left.

ORAZIO: Except that we have some new characters.

EUGENIO: True. No one should see them rehearsing.

ORAZIO: If you want to make the most of an actor, make him a bit scarce; and to show him at his best, you should give him not a long part but a good one.

EUGENIO: And yet there are some actors who beg the poets to write two-thirds of the comedy for them alone.

ORAZIO: A wretched practice. Even when they act well they're boring. And when they're bad they're infuriating.

EUGENIO: Well, we're wasting the hours here and getting nothing done. It appears that my fine companions are not coming.

ORAZIO: You know how actors are: they always rise late.

EUGENIO: Ah, rehearsals are the hardest part of our job.

ORAZIO: Yes, but rehearsals are what make actors good.

EUGENIO: Well, here comes the leading lady.

ORAZIO: Yes, and before everyone else, too! Leading ladies usually like to keep the others waiting.

Scene II

Enter PLACIDA.[3]

PLACIDA: Look, I'm the first one here. Aren't the other ladies going to honor us? Signor Orazio, if they don't come on time, I'm going to leave.

ORAZIO: My dear lady, you've just arrived and already you're upset. Have patience. I've got so much; try to have some yourself.

PLACIDA: I should think you might have sent for me after all the others had arrived.

EUGENIO: *(Aside to* ORAZIO.*)* (You hear? She talks just like a prima donna.)

ORAZIO: (You must be politic; better to bear with her.) My most gracious lady, I asked you to come early, and especially before the others, so that we could discuss together—just the two of us—a matter concerning the direction of our comedies.

PLACIDA: But aren't you the head of the company? Don't you make all the decisions here?

ORAZIO: Yes, I do, but I want everyone to be satisfied with me, and above all you, madam, you who have all my admiration.

EUGENIO: *(Aside to* ORAZIO.*)* (Do you really want to take her advice?)

ORAZIO: *(Aside.)* (First I listen to the advice of others, and then I do exactly as I please.)

PLACIDA: Tell me, Signor Orazio, what comedy have you chosen for tomorrow night?

---

[3] Teodora Medebach, for whom the role of Placida was designed, was noted for her phlegmatic temperament.

ORAZIO: A new one called *A Father His Son's Rival*. Yesterday we rehearsed the first and second acts, and today we shall do the third.

PLACIDA: I'll be happy to rehearse it, but I'm not so sure we can perform it tomorrow night.

EUGENIO: *(Aside to* ORAZIO.*)* (Do you hear? She doesn't agree.)

ORAZIO: (Just wait. She'll come to reason!) May I ask you what other comedy in your opinion would be better to perform?

PLACIDA: Well, the author who provides our comedies has written sixteen of them this year, all new, all character comedies, all of them written out. Why not do one of them?

EUGENIO: Sixteen comedies in a single year! Why that's impossible.

ORAZIO: Yes, he really did. He promised he'd write them and he did, all sixteen.

EUGENIO: Then tell me. What are the titles of these sixteen plays he wrote in one year?

PLACIDA: Let me list them for you. *The Comic Theatre, Women's Ambitions, The Coffee House, The Liar, The Flatterer, The Poets, Pamela, The Man of Taste, The Gambler, The True Friend, The False Invalid, The Cautious Woman, The Unknown Woman Persecuted by the Bumptious Braggart, The Honorable Adventurer, The Fickle Woman,* and *Women's Gossip,*[4] a Venetian comedy.

---

[4] The Italian titles are as follows: *Il teatro comico, I puntigli delle donne, La bottega del caffè, Il bugiardo, L'adulatore, I poeti, La Pamela, Il cavalier di buon gusto, Il giuocatore, Il vero amico, La finta ammalata, La donna prudente, L'incognita perseguitata dal bravo impertinente, L'avventuriere onorato, La donna volubile, I pettegolezzi delle donne.*

EUGENIO: But how about the play we're presenting tomorrow night? Didn't our author write that as well?

ORAZIO: Yes, but it's only a little farce he doesn't bother to count among these comedies.

PLACIDA: But why do you want to do this farce instead of one of the better comedies?

ORAZIO: My dear, you know we are lacking two serious parts, a man and a woman. We're waiting for them now, and if they don't appear we can't do character comedies.

PLACIDA: Well, if we have to do *commedia dell' arte* we'll be in a fine state! People are bored with always seeing the same thing and always hearing the same words. The audience knows what Harlequin will say even before he opens his mouth. As for me, good sir, I warn you that I'll have little to do with these old-fashioned comedies. I'm in love with the new style and nothing else will suit me. Be that as it may, I shall not disappoint you tomorrow evening. Perhaps we won't be giving a character comedy, but at least the actors will be properly directed and the sentiments will be well handled. But if the company is not completed soon, then you can do without me.

ORAZIO: But in the meantime . . .

PLACIDA: Come, come, sir, I have been on my feet quite long enough. I'm going to my dressing room to sit down. When you are ready to rehearse, call me. And tell the other women that it is not the custom for the leading lady to be kept waiting.   *Leaves.*

Scene III

ORAZIO *and* EUGENIO.

EUGENIO: I'm splitting with laughter.

ORAZIO: Go ahead, laugh. I'd sooner curse.

EUGENIO: But weren't you just telling us to have patience?

ORAZIO: Yes, patience, but it doesn't stop the poison from eating me up.

EUGENIO: Here comes Pantalone.

ORAZIO: My good man, do me a favor: go tell the women to hurry along.

EUGENIO: All right, but I can tell you already they'll either be in bed or at their dressing tables. That's all they have on their minds: resting and making themselves beautiful.

Leaves.

Scene IV

ORAZIO, *then* TONINO.[5]

ORAZIO: A good morning to you, Signor Tonino.

TONINO: My most revered master.

ORAZIO: What's the matter? You look disturbed.

TONINO: I don't know myself. Such a tremor I feel all through me, like when the fever's caught you.

ORAZIO: Let me feel your pulse.

TONINO: Yes, my friend, and tell me whether it's beating in single or triple time.

ORAZIO: You have no fever, but your pulse is very agitated; something must be bothering you.

TONINO: You know what it is? Such a fright I don't know where I'm standing?

ORAZIO: Frightened? Of what?

TONINO: My dear Orazio, let's put aside the joking and talk seriously. These character comedies have turned our profession upside down. A poor player who has learned

[5] Tonino speaks in Venetian dialect here, as does Pantalone in the *commedia dell' arte*. Goldoni provides footnotes containing Italian glosses for some terms, such as *tremazzo* (Ital. *tremore*, "tremor"), below.

his craft in the *commedia dell' arte* and who is used to spilling out whatever pops into his head, now he finds himself forced to study books and say what somebody else has thought up; if he has a reputation to worry about, he must wear his brains out memorizing, and every time a new comedy comes along he's afraid that either he won't know it well enough or he won't play his part as he's supposed to.

ORAZIO: Of course this way of acting requires more work and attention, but just think of the greater fame actors have now. And tell me something else, with all your performances in *commedia dell' arte* would you have ever been applauded as much as you were in *The Prudent Man*, *The Advocate*, *The Venetian Twins*,[6] and all the other plays in which our poet chose Pantalone for the leading role?

TONINO: Yes, I know and I'm very happy, but I still can't help being scared. I always feel it's too big a step to take; as Tasso says,

> *To flights that are too sudden and too steep*
> *Oft are there neighbor chasms e'er so deep.*

ORAZIO: Oh, so you know Tasso? Obviously you're well acquainted with Venice if you know Tasso. Here they recite him almost everywhere.

TONINO: Oh, as far as Venice goes, I know my way around.

ORAZIO: Did you enjoy yourself here as a young man?

TONINO: Ha! You're asking me! I had my share, don't you worry!

---

[6] *L'uomo prudente, L'avvocato, Due gemelli.* The first (Bettinelli) edition of 1751 speaks also of *Il vero amico, I poeti, L'avventuriere,* "and many others"; but by the edition of 1761 only those plays enacted by the current Pantalone, an actor named Collalto, were mentioned.

ORAZIO: And how did you make out with the pretty Venetian girls?

TONINO: *Of all those women in my heart impressed*
The most respected memories do rest.

ORAZIO: Marvelous, Pantalone, I like your verve, your joviality. I've heard you sing many a time.

TONINO: Right, sir. I always sing when I'm penniless.

ORAZIO: Do me a favor, while we're waiting for our beloved colleagues to honor us with their presence, will you sing something for me?

TONINO: After I've studied for three hours you want me to sing? I'm sorry, sir, but I just can't do it.

ORAZIO: Come, come. We're alone here and no one will hear you.

TONINO: I can't, honestly. Some other time.

ORAZIO: Just this once. I'm anxious to hear if you're in good voice.

TONINO: And if I am, then will you want me to sing at performances?

ORAZIO: Why not?

TONINO: I'll tell you why not. I play Pantalone, not the musician; if I had wanted to be a musician I'd never have put up with this beard.[7]   *Leaves.*

Scene V

ORAZIO, *then* VITTORIA.

ORAZIO: He only talks that way, but actually he's very agreeable. If need be, I'm sure he'll sing.

VITTORIA: My respects, Signor Orazio.

[7] *Here the spectators applauded repeatedly and forced the actor to sing; such being the Author's expectation at this point.*

ORAZIO: Oh, my dear Signora Vittoria, your most humble servant: you are one of the most diligent in the company.

VITTORIA: I always do my duty willingly, and to show you I mean what I say, look at this: since my part in our play today is so small, look, I've picked up another and I'm studying it now.

ORAZIO: Wonderful, that's the spirit. Which one is it?

VITTORIA: This is Catte's part in *The Honest Wench*.

ORAZIO: Aha! So you like that role of a sweet little fleecer? [8]

VITTORIA: When I'm on stage I do, but not when I'm *off* stage.

ORAZIO: Well, be it a little or a lot, women always love to pluck.

VITTORIA: There was once a time when the plucking was good, but now we've run out of roosters.

ORAZIO: And yet you can still find young men who have been plucked to the bone.

VITTORIA: Would you like to know why? I'll tell you. To begin with, they have hardly any feathers left; then after one feather goes for gambling, another for gluttony, one for the theatres, one for festivities, we poor women are left with nothing but dull pinfeathers, and often we're the ones who must re-dress our poor, plucked roosters.

ORAZIO: And have you ever re-dressed one yourself?

VITTORIA: Oh, I'm no one's fool.

ORAZIO: To be sure, you know your way around, you're an actress.

---

[8] In the original, *pelarina*. Goldoni's note reads: *A Lombard term applied to women who are skilled in extracting gifts.* (*Pelarina*, from Italian *pelare*, "to peel or pluck"; Goldoni had written a popular musical intermezzo named *La Pelarina*, in which the leading lady was a virtuoso singer.)

VITTORIA: I know my way around just enough not to be duped. As for being an actress, there are plenty of other women who never go anywhere, there are plenty of wives who sit at home and know a hundred times more than us.

ORAZIO: In other words, to be clever one needs only to be a woman.

VITTORIA: That's right, and do you know what makes women clever?

ORAZIO: What?

VITTORIA: Men. They're the ones that teach us cunning.

ORAZIO: So if it weren't for men, women would be pure innocence.

VITTORIA: Without a doubt.

ORAZIO: And if it weren't for you women, we men would have remained innocent.

VITTORIA: Oh, you wretched scoundrels!

ORAZIO: Oh, you sly wenches!

VITTORIA: Come now, why are we waiting here? Are we going to rehearse or not?

ORAZIO: We still need Harlequin, Brighella, and the ladies.

Scene VI

Enter ANSELMO.[9]

ANSELMO: Brighella is here, at your service.

ORAZIO: Oh, excellent.

ANSELMO: I've just been talking to a poet.

---

[9] Anselmo speaks Venetian here, as does Brighella in the *commedia dell' arte.*

ORAZIO: Poet? What kind of poet?

ANSELMO: A comic poet.

VITTORIA: Is his name by chance Signor Lelio?

ANSELMO: That's right, Signor Lelio.

VITTORIA: He called on me as well, and the moment I saw him I could tell he was a poet.

ORAZIO: How is that?

VITTORIA: Because he was penniless and cheerful.

ORAZIO: These are the marks of a poet?

VITTORIA: That's right, sir. When poets fall into poverty they divert themselves with the Muses to keep happy.

ANSELMO: And they're not the only ones.

ORAZIO: Who else then?

ANSELMO: Actors.

VITTORIA: True, true. When they have no money they sell and pawn everything to be cheerful.

ANSELMO: There are some actors loaded down with debts and yet they'll march as intrepidly as paladins.

ORAZIO: Come, my friends, you do yourselves injustice speaking like this. Throughout the acting profession you will find, unfortunately, some scoundrels; but the world has plenty of these, and in every art there will be some. An actor should be honorable like everyone else; he should know his duty, love honor and all the moral virtues.

ANSELMO: But there's one virtue they can never have.

ORAZIO: And what's that?

ANSELMO: Thrift.

VITTORIA: Just like a poet.

ORAZIO: And yet if there is anyone who needs thrift it's an actor. His profession is subject to endless vicissitudes; profit is always uncertain and misfortunes frequent.

ANSELMO: Well, shall we hear this poet?

ORAZIO: But we don't need one.

ANSELMO: That doesn't matter; let's just hear what he has to say.

ORAZIO: No. It's not right to hear him out of mere curiosity. We ought to show respect for learned men. But since you proposed him to me I'll gladly hear him, and if he has any good ideas I won't hesitate to accept them.

VITTORIA: But won't our own author take offense?

ORAZIO: Not at all, I know him well. He would take offense if this Signor Lelio wanted to mistreat his plays; but if he has manners and is a sage and discreet critic, I'm sure they will make good friends.

ANSELMO: Then I'll go bring him in.

ORAZIO: Yes, and please inform the others to come hear him. I like everyone to speak his opinion. Though actors can't compose plays, they can still tell the good from the bad.

ANSELMO: Yes, but some try to judge a comedy only by their own part. If their part is short they say the play is bad; they all want to play the lead. An actor is satisfied only when he hears laughter and applause.

For if the people laugh and gladly plaud
Then is the actor worthy of their laud. *Leaves.*

Scene VII

ORAZIO *and* VITTORIA.

ORAZIO: Here we are again with the same old couplets. At one time every scene ended that way.

VITTORIA: That's right, every dialogue finished with a jingle. The players all used to become poets.

ORAZIO: Nowadays tastes in comedies have changed and these verses are used with moderation.

VITTORIA: Ah! Such innovations have come to the comic theatre!

ORAZIO: In your opinion, do you feel that the man who brought these changes has done a good thing?

VITTORIA: Well, I'm hardly the one to answer this, but seeing how people applaud, I think he did more good than harm. But let's say that for us it's bad, since we must study more, and for you it's good, because it makes your cash box heavier.   *Leaves.*

Scene VIII

ORAZIO, *then* GIANNI.[10]

ORAZIO: People are always counting what I take in but never what I pay out. If a lean year comes along, Heaven help our poor director. Ah, here comes Harlequin.

GIANNI: Signor Orazio, since I have the honor of favoring you with my insufficiency, I have come thus to receive the discomfort of your graces.

ORAZIO: Hurrah for Gianni! *(Aside.)* (I can't tell if he's speaking as the second Zanni[11] or if he thinks he's speaking correctly.)

---

[10] Gianni speaks Venetian (or a Bergamese variant), as does Harlequin in the *commedia dell' arte. Navicella,* "little vessel," below, is a more purely Italian word, and hence conspicuous in his speech.

[11] *In actors' jargon Harlequin was called the second Zanni* [the Venetian form of Gianni or Giovanni] *and Brighella the first Zanni.*

GIANNI: I was told to come to the disconcert and I haven't failed. In fact, I was in the coffeehouse and to make haste I broke my cup out of kindness to you.

ORAZIO: I'm sorry for being the cause of your misfortune.

GIANNI: Don't worry. It's nothing at all. *Post factum nullum consilium.*[12]

ORAZIO: *(Aside.)* (He's in a fine mood, all right!) Tell me, Gianni, how do you like Venice?

GIANNI: I don't.

ORAZIO: No! Why not?

GIANNI: Because last night I fell into the Grand Canal.

ORAZIO: Oh, my poor Gianni, how did you do that?

GIANNI: Just let me tell you: since the little vessel . . .

ORAZIO: Oh, I didn't know you spoke Tuscan!

GIANNI: Why all the time, lickety-split.

ORAZIO: But that's not the way a second Zanni speaks.

GIANNI: My good man, will you tell me in what tongue a second Zanni is supposed to speak?

ORAZIO: He ought to speak Bergamese.

GIANNI: He ought to! I too know that he *ought* to, but how *does* he speak?

ORAZIO: I really couldn't tell you.

GIANNI: Then first go and learn how Harlequins speak before you come here to correct us. *(Singing in a lively voice.)* La lara, la lara, la ra.

ORAZIO: *(Aside.)* (He can still make me laugh.) Tell me: how did you happen to fall in the water?

GIANNI: While disembarking from the gondola I placed one foot on shore and the other on the deck. The gondola left shore and I, from a Bergamese, was baptized a Venetian.

---

[12] "After the deed, [there is] no [room for] advice."

ORAZIO: Gianni, tomorrow evening we must be on stage with a new play.

GIANNI: Well, I'm ready: stomach in, chest out, chin up. Nothing to worry about!

ORAZIO: Remember, we're no longer acting in the old style.

GIANNI: All right, we'll act in the new style.

ORAZIO: Now there is a revival of good taste.

GIANNI: The Bergamese know what's good, too.

ORAZIO: And audiences are not easily satisfied.

GIANNI: If you keep intimidating me like this I won't put one foot on stage. I play a character who's supposed to make people laugh, but how can I make people laugh if I can't laugh myself, if I have to go through all this thinking and trembling? Audience, I beg only one thing of you, I implore you my dearest, my most sympathetic audience, please, for the sake of charity and courtesy, if you want to honor me with a few dozen apples would you kindly throw them cooked instead of raw.[13]

ORAZIO: I appreciate your frankness, Gianni. Anyone else would be accused of being too brash, but for Harlequin, who, as you say, is expected to make others laugh, this joviality and boldness is all to the good.

GIANNI: *Audaces fortuna juvat, timidosque,*[14] and so on and so forth.

ORAZIO: In a few minutes I must interview a poet, and then I want to rehearse some scenes.

GIANNI: If it's a poet you need, here I am.

ORAZIO: Are you also a poet?

---

[13] *In Venice baked apples are sold in the theatres in the evening.*

[14] "Fortune aids the bold, and [rejects] the timid"; cf. Cicero, *Tusculan Disputations*, ii.4.11; Virgil, *Aeneid*, x.284.

GIANNI: Oh, am I!

> Three times mad is my position,
> Poet, painter and musician.

Leaves.

ORAZIO: Good, very good. That one I like very much. In a Harlequin even rhymes are bearable. But where are those players? I'll go hurry them along. You need a great deal of patience to direct a company. If you don't believe me, try it yourself for a week and I guarantee you'll lose your enthusiasm. *Leaves.*

Scene IX

Enter BEATRICE *and* PETRONIO.

BEATRICE: Come, Doctor, do me this honor. I have picked you to be my gentleman in waiting.

PETRONIO: Oh, Heaven forbid!

BEATRICE: Why do you say that?

PETRONIO: In the first place, I am not so insane as to subject myself to the bizarre moods of a woman. Secondly, if I did, I would choose someone outside the company, since I've enough sense not to foul my own nest. And thirdly, if I ever were your gentleman in waiting I would be playing the very part of the Doctor in the play called *Her Husband's Mother.*

BEATRICE: What do you mean by that?

PETRONIO: In compensation for my submission I would receive only disdain.[15]

---

[15] In the earlier editions, "only a glass of water in my face."

BEATRICE: Now look, I attach no importance to this sort of thing. I have never had a gentleman in waiting nor do I want one now; but should it ever be necessary I'd insist he be young.

PETRONIO: Women always cling to the worst they can find.

BEATRICE: What one likes is never the worst.

PETRONIO: You should seek not what you like but what does you good.

BEATRICE: Indeed, you are good only at offering advice.

PETRONIO: Evidently I am better at offering it than you are at taking it.

BEATRICE: I'll have plenty of time for that when I grow old.

PETRONIO: *Principiis obsta: sero medicina paratur.*[16]

Scene X

Enter EUGENIO, ORAZIO, PLACIDA.

BEATRICE: Good day to you, Signora Placida.

PLACIDA: My respects to Signora Beatrice.

BEATRICE: How are you? Are you well?

PLACIDA: Quite well, by your leave. And you, how are you?

BEATRICE: Oh, not at my best. A bit worn out from the journey.

PLACIDA: These journeys are such an ordeal!

BEATRICE: Ha! They make me laugh when they say we do nothing but travel about amusing ourselves.

---

[16] "Hesitate at the beginning: it is too late when the medicine is prepared [after the disease has flourished]" (Ovid, *Remedies of Love*, 91–92).

PLACIDA: Some amusement! We eat badly and sleep worse, we suffer first the heat and then the cold. I could easily do without this kind of amusement.

EUGENIO: Well, my ladies, have you finished with your compliments?

PLACIDA: My compliments are quickly done with.

BEATRICE: Nor do I stand on ceremony.

ORAZIO: Let's sit down then. Servants, where are you? Bring some chairs here. *(SERVANTS bring chairs and all are seated, the ladies next to each other.)* We are going to hear a new poet now.

PLACIDA: I'll be delighted.

EUGENIO: Here he comes.

PETRONIO: Oh, poor man! He's so very thin!

Scene XI

Enter LELIO.

LELIO: Your most humble servant, ladies and gentlemen. *(All greet him.)* Will you be so kind as to inform me which of these ladies plays the lead?

ORAZIO: Here she is, Signora Placida.

LELIO: *(Kisses her hand.)* Allow me, with all reverence, to perform my duty and offer you my respects.

PLACIDA: You do me too much honor, sir, I don't deserve it.

LELIO: *(To BEATRICE.)* And you, madam, might you be the second lady?

BEATRICE: At your service.

LELIO: *(As above.)* Allow me, with you also, to . . .

BEATRICE: *(Withdrawing her hand.)* Why, you needn't.

LELIO: *(Tries again.)* I implore you . . .

BEATRICE: *(As above.)* Pray, don't bother.

LELIO: But it is my duty.

BEATRICE: As you wish.   *(He kisses her hand.)*

ORAZIO: *(To* EUGENIO.*)* This poet is extremely ceremonious.

EUGENIO: *(To* ORAZIO.*)* Most poets act this way with women.

ORAZIO: You are, then, Signor Lelio, the celebrated composer of comedies, if I am not mistaken?

LELIO: At your command. And who is your worship, if you will allow me?

ORAZIO: I play the part of the first *amoroso*, and am also the head of the company.

LELIO: Permit me, then, to discharge my duty to you as well.
                    (Pays his respects affectedly.)

ORAZIO: Please, don't trouble yourself. Hey there, give this man a chair.

LELIO: You honor me with excessive kindness.
          *(*SERVANTS *bring a chair and leave.)*

ORAZIO: Do sit down.

LELIO: Now, if you will allow me, I'll move a little closer to these damsels.

ORAZIO: You enjoy the company of ladies.

LELIO: As you can see. The Muses are ladies. Long live the fair sex! Long live the fair sex!

PETRONIO: My good poet, your servant.

LELIO: Your slave. My master, pray who are you?

PETRONIO: The Doctor, by your leave.

LELIO: Oh, this gives me extreme pleasure. I have an excellent play made just for you.

PETRONIO: What is it called?

LELIO: *The Ignorant Doctor.*

PETRONIO: As a matter of fact, I, too, delight in composing, and have written a play.

LELIO: Oh yes? What is it called?

PETRONIO: *The Mad Poet.*

LELIO: Bravo, Doctor, bravo! *(To* PLACIDA.*)* Madam, I have some tender scenes made just for you; not only will the audience cry, but their very chairs will break out in tears. *(To* BEATRICE.*)* And madam, for you I have some scenes with such fervor that even the balcony will stand up and applaud.

EUGENIO: *(Aside.)* (They haven't made poets like this for over a century! He has the seats shedding tears and the balcony clapping hands!)

ORAZIO: Would you give us the pleasure of hearing one of your excellent works?

LELIO: Here is an improvised comedy that I wrote in three-quarters of an hour.

PETRONIO: I dare say that it was made a bit helter-skelter-slap-dashedly.

LELIO: Just listen to the title: *Pantalone the Amorous Father, with Harlequin the Faithful Servant, Brighella Mediator for the Sake of Money, Ottavio the Administrator Within His Villa, and Rosaura Delirious with Love. (To the women.)* Ah, what do you think? Isn't it marvelous? Do you like it?

PLACIDA: The title's so long that I've already forgotten it.

BEATRICE: Well, it does mention everyone in the company.

LELIO: That's exactly what one must do: write a title which is itself the subject of the play.

ORAZIO: Forgive me, Signor Lelio, but a good play should

have unity of action; it must have only one subject and the title must be simple.

LELIO: Very well, but too much is always better than too little. My comedy has five titles; choose whichever you like best. In fact, do it this way: each year that you produce it, change the title, and for five years you will have a comedy that is always new.

ORAZIO: Let us proceed and hear how it begins.

LELIO: *(To* PLACIDA.*)* Ah, madam, it will be my great pleasure to have the honor to compose something for you.

PLACIDA: I'm afraid I will not do you honor.

LELIO: *(To* BEATRICE.*)* Oh, I so admire your attributes! You were born to play the tyrannical beauty.

BEATRICE: My dear poet, you are mocking me.

LELIO: I say it with all my heart.

PETRONIO: I beg your pardon, Signor Lelio, but have you ever acted?

LELIO: Yes, I have acted in the most celebrated academies of Italy.

PETRONIO: It seems to me that your worship is perfectly suited to scenes of caricature.

ORAZIO: Well, sir, may we hear this subject?

LELIO: Yes, sir, by your leave I'll begin: *Act One: The Street; Pantalone and the Doctor; Scene of Friendship.*

ORAZIO: Old-fashioned! Old-fashioned!

LELIO: But please, just listen a moment. *The Doctor asks Pantalone for the hand of his daughter.*

EUGENIO: And Pantalone promises it to him.

LELIO: Precisely! Precisely! *And Pantalone promises it to him. The Doctor withdraws. Pantalone knocks, calling Rosaura.*

ORAZIO: And Rosaura comes out on the street.

LELIO: Right you are, sir: *And Rosaura comes out on the street.*

ORAZIO: *(Rising.)* With your permission, I'd rather hear no more.

LELIO: But why? What's wrong with it?

ORAZIO: This enormous impropriety of having women come out on the streets has been tolerated in Italy for many years at the expense of decorum. But thank Heaven we have corrected this, we have abolished it, and it will no longer be permitted on our stage.

LELIO: Then let's try it another way: *Pantalone enters Rosaura's house and the Doctor remains on the street.*

ORAZIO: And while Pantalone is inside what will you have the Doctor say?

LELIO: *While Pantalone is inside, the Doctor says* ... why, *the Doctor says whatever he pleases. At this point*—Oh, listen to this! *At this point Harlequin, servant to the Doctor, comes up ever so quietly and clubs his master.*

ORAZIO: Oh dear! Oh dear! It gets worse and worse!

PETRONIO: If the poet played the Doctor, the joke might go over.

ORAZIO: It's an indignity for a servent to club his master. Unfortunately, actors used to carry on this sort of slapstick, but now it is no longer done. What could be more foolish? Harlequin clubbing his master, and his master tolerating it simply because he's good-natured! My dear poet, if you have nothing more modern than this, I beg you not to trouble yourself any further.

LELIO: But you must at least listen to this gem of dialogue.

ORAZIO: Very well. Let's listen to this gem of dialogue.

LELIO: *First dialogue. Man pleads. Woman rejects. Man:*

Deafer you than tempest blust'ring, hear you not my plaintive suff'ring! Woman: Away, let me be, oh fie! You insolent gnat, you gad-fly. Man: My idol, my beloved . . .

ORAZIO: No more! Please, no more!

LELIO: *Have compassion, I beseech . . .*

ORAZIO: Go sing your verses in the streets.[17]   *Leaves.*

LELIO: *Woman: The more you adore me, the more I abhor thee. Man: Barbarous ungrateful heart.*

EUGENIO: I too am ready to part.   *Leaves.*

LELIO: *Woman: Begone with your love insane, you beseech me in vain. Man: Hear me, oh woman, oh Cassiopeia . . .*

PETRONIO: Help! Help! He's given me diarrhea!   *Leaves.*

LELIO: *Woman: Flee! Fly! Vanish! Man: No more, oh cruel, oh stony heart!*

BEATRICE: Let me depart! Let me depart!   *Leaves.*

LELIO: *My bosom you pierce, so sad.*

PLACIDA: You, my poet, are stark raving mad!   *Leaves.*

LELIO: *Woman: Beg not for my compassion since pity I'll deny. Man: If pity you won't grant me, desperate I shall die.* What? They're all gone? They've left *me* here alone? Is this the way they scorn a man of my quality? I swear to Heaven I'll have my revenge. I'll show them who I am. I'll have my plays performed in spite of them, and if I find no other place I'll stage them on a platform in the piazza with a company of perfectly good charlatans. What presumption these people have, thinking they can remake the Comic Theatre overnight! Just because they have presented a few comedies they feel entitled to do away

[17] Literally, "Go sing your verses to the *colascione*"—a bulky two- or three-stringed lute to which crude verses were commonly sung.

with all the old ones? I tell you they'll never succeed. With all their innovations they'll never make half the money that *Don Juan* made for so many years.[18]

[18] Literally, *The Great Stone Guest. Il gran convitato di pietra* was an Italian version of the Don Juan story.

Act Two

Scene I

LELIO *and* ANSELMO.

LELIO: Signor Anselmo, I'm desperate.

ANSELMO: But my dear man, you come here and you propose such a rag of a subject that even a company of puppets would refuse to act it.

LELIO: Well, I won't insist about the subject, but they never should have ripped the dialogue apart that way.

ANSELMO: But don't you understand that dialogues, witticisms, soliloquies, insults, conceits, lamentations, tirades, and such are no longer used?

LELIO: Then what do they use these days?

ANSELMO: Character comedies.

LELIO: Well, in that case I have as many character comedies as you wish.

ANSELMO: Then why didn't you propose one to our director?

LELIO: I had no idea that Italians liked character comedies.

ANSELMO: Why, this is the only kind of play Italians want nowadays; and what is more, in no time at all these character comedies have so improved everyone's taste that now even common people have definite opinions about whether a play is well or badly written.

LELIO: This is remarkable indeed!

ANSELMO: And let me tell you why. Comedy was created to correct vice and ridicule bad customs; when the ancient poets wrote comedies in this manner, the common people could participate, because, seeing the copy of a character on stage, each found the original either in himself or in someone else. But when comedies became merely ridiculous, no one paid attention any more, because with the excuse of making people laugh, they admitted the worst and most blatant errors. But now that we have returned to fish comedies from nature's *Mare Magnum*, men feel their hearts touched again. They can identify with the characters or passions and discern whether a character is well observed and developed, and whether a passion is well motivated.

LELIO: You sound more like a poet than an actor.

ANSELMO: I'll tell you, sir. With the mask I'm Brighella, without the mask I'm a man who may not have enough invention to be a poet, but at least has enough discernment to understand his own craft. An ignorant actor never plays any character well.

LELIO: *(Aside.)* (I'm afraid these players know much more than I do.) My dear friend, would you be so kind as to go tell your director that I have some character comedies?

ANSELMO: I'll do that, and you can return either tonight or tomorrow morning when I'll surely have spoken to him.

LELIO: No, my time is short and I'd rather do it now.

ANSELMO: But you see, sir, we have to arrange some scenes now, and there won't be time enough.

LELIO: If he can't hear me immediately I'll go and offer my comedies to some other company.

ANSELMO: Do as you like, sir. We've no need of them.

LELIO: But your theatre will lose a great opportunity.

ANSELMO: Well, we'll simply have to bear it.

LELIO: Tomorrow I must leave, and if he doesn't hear me now it will be too late.

ANSELMO: Then go, and a pleasant journey to you.

LELIO: My friend, to tell you the truth, I'm without money and honestly don't know where my next meal is coming from.

ANSELMO: Now this is more convincing.

LELIO: I'm depending on you to speak in my favor.

ANSELMO: Let me go to Orazio now. Maybe he'll come right away to hear what you have to offer in the way of characters. *(Aside.)* (But if you ask me the best character for comedy is his very own: the hungry poet.) *Leaves.*

Scene II

LELIO, *then* PLACIDA.

LELIO: I couldn't have come at a worse time. Today players are enlightened. But I mustn't let this stop me. Wit and boldness. Perhaps I can manage to win them over with imposture. Ah, here comes the leading lady again. I think I have made some impression on her.

PLACIDA: Signor Lelio, still here?

LELIO: Yes, my lady, like a charmed moth I fly circles around the light of your pupils.

PLACIDA: Sir, if you insist on this style you're going to make a fool of yourself.

LELIO: But aren't your commonplace books[19] filled with such conceits?

[19] *Generici*, or guidebooks for *commedia dell' arte* actors, containing stock soliloquies, dialogues, tirades, etc.

PLACIDA: I've burned all such books, and so have the rest of the players enlightened by the new style. For the most part we perform premeditated character comedies; but when it happens that we make improvised speeches we use a familiar, natural, and easy style, so as not to stray from what is plausible.

LELIO: In that case I'll give you plays written in a style so refined that in studying them you will be utterly enchanted.

PLACIDA: Provided they are not in the old-fashioned style full of *antitheses* and *metaphors*.

LELIO: Do not *antitheses*, perhaps, make pleasant listening? Is not the juxtaposition of words delectable to the ear?

PLACIDA: As long as the *antithesis* remains a *figure of speech* it's all right, but when it becomes a *bad habit* it is insufferable.

LELIO: Men of my intelligence know how to draw *figures of speech* from *bad habits*, and if I so please I can render a pretty figure of *repetition* out of the most ordinary *cacophony*.

PLACIDA: I'd be happy to hear one of these witty creations of yours.

LELIO: Ah madam, you must be my queen, my guiding star, my goddess.

PLACIDA: Why, this *figure* is a *hyperbole*.

LELIO: With my most subtle *rhetoric* I will investigate all the *topics*[20] of your heart.

---

[20] *Luoghi topici*—"commonplaces," or Greek *topoi*—were the conventional motifs with which rhetoricians formed their compositions, frequently with little concern for relevance or coherence, as in the dialogue which follows here.

PLACIDA: *(Aside.)* (I wouldn't want his *rhetoric* to probe any further!)

LELIO: From your beauty I *deduce philosophically* your goodness.

PLACIDA: You seem a better *mathematician* than a *philosopher*.

LELIO: I will be a *speculative* observer of the prerogatives that come from your excellent qualities.

PLACIDA: You are mistaken in the *calculation*; you are a bad *arithmetician*.

LELIO: I hope that with the perfection of *optics* I can *speculate* on your beauty.

PLACIDA: In this, as well, you are a poor *astrologer*.

LELIO: Will you not be the amorous physician of my wounds?

PLACIDA: Do you know what I shall be? A *judge of assizes*, who will have you bound and conducted to the madhouse. *(Aside.)* (If I stay here any longer I'll become as mad as he is. He's making me speak puns which are as much outlawed as dueling pistols.)   *Leaves.*

Scene III

LELIO, *then* ORAZIO.

LELIO: These princesses of the theatre try to lord it over the poets, but if it weren't for us they'd never hear a single clap from the audience. But here comes the director. I must use the humble approach with him. Oh hunger! Oh hunger! How painful you can be!

ORAZIO: Brighella tells me that your honor has some character comedies. I don't need any, but I'll take some just the same to please you.

LELIO: I shall be eternally obliged to you.

ORAZIO: Bring in some chairs.

(SERVANTS *bring in two chairs and leave.*)

LELIO: *(Aside.)* (Fortune, be kind to me!)

ORAZIO: Will you be so kind as to show me one of your fine works?

LELIO: Here we are. This is a play translated from the French and called . . .

ORAZIO: Wait. Don't say any more. If it's a translation I've no use for it.

LELIO: Why not? Don't you like French works?

ORAZIO: On the contrary; I praise them, esteem them, venerate them; but they don't suit my needs. The French have triumphed in the art of drama for an entire century; I think the time has come for Italy to show the world that the germ of those good authors, who, after the Greeks and Romans, were the first to enrich and ennoble the theatre, is still alive. One cannot deny that in their plays the French have created fine and well-depicted characters, that the passions are well handled and the ideas are keen and witty and brilliant; but their public is satisfied with very little. An entire French play can rest on the shoulders of a single character. Around one single passion—of course, well developed throughout the play—they spin out dialogue upon dialogue, conveying an air of novelty by mere strength of expression. Our Italians demand much more. They expect that the principal character be strong, original, and recognizable; that virtually all the figures in the episodes be characters in their own right; that the plot be reasonably rich in surprises and innovations. They want the moral mixed with the spice of jokes and banter. They want an unexpected ending, yet one deriving from the play in its entirety. Their demands are too numerous to list; and only with experience, practice, and time can we ever come to know them and satisfy them.

LELIO: But once a play contains all these good qualities, will everyone in Italy like it?

ORAZIO: No, by no means. Every individual has his own peculiar manner of thinking, and this will naturally affect his reaction to any given play. If he's melancholy he won't like jokes; if jolly, he won't like moralizing. For this reason plays have never had, and never will have, universal appeal. Nevertheless, when a play is good most people like it, and when it's bad nearly everyone dislikes it.

LELIO: In that case I have a character comedy of my own invention that I'm sure most people will like. I think I've followed all the rules; but if I haven't, I've certainly observed the most essential one which is unity of place.

ORAZIO: Whoever told you that unity of place was an essential rule?

LELIO: Aristotle.

ORAZIO: Have you read Aristotle?

LELIO: To tell you the truth, I haven't, but I've heard this from others.

ORAZIO: Let me explain to you what Aristotle says. The philosopher began to write about comedy but never finished, and all we have from him on this subject are a few imperfect pages. In his *Poetics* he prescribed unity of place for tragedy, but for comedy he said nothing. Some say that what he said for tragedy must be understood for comedy as well, and that had he finished his treatise on comedy he would have prescribed unity of place. But it can be objected that if Aristotle were still alive, he himself would do away with an arduous rule which has begotten a thousand absurdities, a thousand improprieties and blunders. I distinguish between two types of comedy: *simple comedy* and *plotted comedy*. *Simple comedy* can be staged with a single set; *plotted comedy* cannot be done this way without stiffness and incongruity. The ancients did not have our facilities for changing scenes, and for this reason they observed the unity. We should observe it if the comedy takes place in the same city, and all the more so if it takes place in the same house, provided, however, the characters don't suddenly leap from Naples to Castille as they used to in some Spanish plays—though nowadays they are beginning to correct such an abuse and have scruples about distance and time. I conclude, therefore, that if a comedy can be presented without forced devices or incongruities in a single setting, then we should do so; but if for the sake of unity of place we must introduce absurdities, then it is better to change settings and respect the rule of verisimilitude.

LELIO: And to think I tried so hard to observe this unity.

ORAZIO: Well, it might be appropriate. What is the title of your comedy?

LELIO: *A Father His Daughters' Pander.*

ORAZIO: Dear me! It's a bad subject. When the protagonist of a comedy is a man of loose morals, either his character must change for the better, or the comedy will be nothing less than wicked.

LELIO: But shouldn't we put sinful characters on the stage in order to correct and shame them?

ORAZIO: Sinful characters, yes, but not scandalous ones as in the case of a father who pimps for his own daughters.

Furthermore, when we want to introduce a sinful character we should not place him in the very center of the
action, but instead relegate him to one side, which is to
say, to episodes where he can be confronted with a
virtuous character. In such a way virtue is truly exalted
and vice truly condemned.

LELIO: I'm at my wit's end, sir. I've nothing else to offer
you.

ORAZIO: I'm infinitely sorry, but I cannot use what you've
shown me.

LELIO: Sir, my misery is without end.

ORAZIO: I regret this deeply, but I don't know how to help
you.

LELIO: I have one thing left to offer you, and I hope your
heart will not let you despise it.

ORAZIO: Tell me, what is it?

LELIO: Myself.

ORAZIO: Yourself? What would I do with you?

LELIO: I wish to offer myself as an actor if you will deign to
accept me.

ORAZIO: *(Rises.)* You want to appear on stage as an actor?
You, a poet who ought to be the instructor of actors,
want to stoop to become an actor yourself? Why, you're
an impostor. From the false poet that you are you will
become a worse actor. I refuse your person as I have
already refused your works, and lastly, I must inform
you that if you think honorable actors like us give shelter
to vagabonds you are greatly deceived.   *Leaves.*

LELIO: The devil burn all subjects, plays and poetry. I
should have said from the beginning that I was an actor.
Now the director rejects me and sends me away. But who
knows? Perhaps he'll come to accept me through

Brighella. In any event, I like the theatre. And if I have no skill at composing, I'll dedicate myself to acting. Like the good soldier who couldn't become a captain and reconciled himself to being a drummer.   *Leaves.*

Scene IV

THE PROMPTER, *holding sheets of paper and a small candle; later* PLACIDA *and* EUGENIO.

PROMPTER: Take heart, ladies, gentlemen, the hour's growing late. Come try out your scenes. *Rosaura* and *Florindo*, it's your turn.

PLACIDA: I'm ready.

EUGENIO: Here I am. *(To* PROMPTER.*)* Go ahead, prompt.

PLACIDA: Do your job well now, Prompter; where I know my part, prompt softly, and where I don't know it, prompt loudly.

PROMPTER: And how am I to know where you know it and where you don't?

PLACIDA: You ought to if you know your craft. Go now, and if you make me fumble, Heaven help you!

PROMPTER: *(Aside.)* (Ah yes, this is just like players. If they don't know their parts, who's to blame but the prompter.)   *(Withdraws and begins to prompt.)*

Scene V

ROSAURA *and* FLORINDO *(*PLACIDA *and* EUGENIO.*)*

ROSAURA: *Dearest Florindo, you wrong me if you doubt my faith. My father cannot bring himself to dispose of my hand.*

FLORINDO: *It is not your father I fear, but my own. It may be that the good Doctor, loving us tenderly, does not wish your ruin; but as for my father, his love for you torments me, and I haven't the heart to declare myself his rival.*

ROSAURA: *But do you think I am so foolish as to give my consent to Signor Pantalone? I said I would be a bride in the house of the Bisognosi, but in my heart I meant the son's bride, not the father's.*

FLORINDO: *And yet he has flattered himself into thinking you will be his, and woe to me if he discovers our correspondence.*

ROSAURA: *I shall conceal my love in a silence which only the fear of losing you can break.*

FLORINDO: *Adieu, my dearest, remain faithful to me!*

ROSAURA: *You are leaving me so soon?*

FLORINDO: *If your father discovers you here, all our secrets will be revealed.*

ROSAURA: *But at this hour he will not return.*

Scene VI

Enter PANTALONE.

PANTALONE: (From within.) *Ho there! Anyone home? May I come in?*

FLORINDO: *Alas! My father!*

ROSAURA: *Hide in that chamber.*

FLORINDO: *Surely he's come to speak love to you.*

ROSAURA: *I'll encourage him so he won't suspect anything.*

FLORINDO: *Encourage him, but only up to a certain point.*

ROSAURA: *Haste! Haste!*

FLORINDO: *Oh fatal love that makes me jealous of my own father!* Withdraws.

PANTALONE: *Is anyone here? May I come in?*

ROSAURA: *Come in, Signor Pantalone, come in.*

PANTALONE: *Rosaura, my precious lady. Are you alone?*

ROSAURA: *Yes, sir, I am alone. My father is away.*

PANTALONE: *Would you mind if I stayed with you a minute, or would you prefer me to leave?*

ROSAURA: *You are welcome to stay or go as you please, sir.*

PANTALONE: *Thank you, my little angel. Blessed be that delightful mouth that speaks such lovely words.*

ROSAURA: *You make me laugh, Signor Pantalone.*

PANTALONE: *Heaven aids the light of heart. I'm pleased that you laugh and are merry, and when I see you so cheerful my own heart leaps.*

ROSAURA: *I suppose you have come to see my father.*

PANTALONE: *Nay, my pillar, nay, my hope. I've come not for your papa but for his little cherub.*

ROSAURA: *And who might this little cherub be?*

PANTALONE: *Ah you rascal! You thief of my heart! You know that I'm wasting away for you, that I'm dying for you.*

ROSAURA: *I am very much obliged for your love.*

PANTALONE: *Let me be frank. We're alone now and no one can hear us. Would it please you, would you deign to join me in marriage?*

ROSAURA: *Sir, we shall have to discuss it with my father.*

PANTALONE: *Your father's a good friend of mine and I hope he won't say no. But it's from you I want to hear; you who are my very viscera, give me just two words to console my poor heart. I would be ever so happy to hear you say, "Why yes, sir, yes, Signor Pantalone, I'll have you, I love you*

very much; even though you're old, I love you very much."
Just tell me this and I'll be happy as a bowl of lasagne.

ROSAURA: *But I don't know how to say such things.*

PANTALONE: *Tell me, my pet, have you ever made love?*

ROSAURA: *No, sir, never.*

PANTALONE: *Don't you know how to make love?*

ROSAURA: *No, in truth I do not.*

PANTALONE: *Then I shall teach you, my dear, I shall teach you.*

ROSAURA: *But at your age, Signor Pantalone, such things are hardly proper.*

PANTALONE: *Love has respect for no one. It wounds the old and the young alike; and in love the old need just as much compassion as the young.*

FLORINDO: *Therefore,* (Enters.) *have compassion also for me, because I too am in love.*

PANTALONE: *What? You here?*

FLORINDO: *Yes, sir, I am here, and for the same purpose that has brought you.*

PANTALONE: *I confess it makes me quiver with rage and shame that my son should discover my weaknesses. And you, my lad, must have a great deal of gall to appear in front of me at such a dangerous moment. But let this surprise, this discovery, serve as a restraint on us both; you for your scheming and me for my passion. To remedy this bad example I'll have you know that I condemn myself, that I confess to having been too weak, too remiss, too mad. And if I said that the old, when in love, deserve just as much compassion as the young, it was because I was carried away by the fervor of love. On the contrary, an elder who has children should not fall in love at the expense of his own family. Likewise, a son should not set his affections on a woman without the consent of the man who put him into the world. Hence, both of us, out of this house! Me, by choice, you, by obedience. Me, to remedy the scandal that I have brought upon you, you to learn to live with more prudence, judgment, and respect for your father.*

FLORINDO: *But sir . . .*

PANTALONE: *Begone, I tell you, leave this house!*

FLORINDO: *Pray, allow me to . . .*

PANTALONE: *Obey, or I will drag you down these stairs with my own hands.*

FLORINDO: (Aside.) *(Oh, damned be this jealousy that made me so impatient!)* Leaves.

PANTALONE: *Rosaura, my dear, I don't know what to say. I loved you, I still love you, and I always will love you. But one moment alone has decided our lives. Your life, which will never again be tormented by this miserable old man; my life, which will soon come to an end, sacrificed for the sake of my propriety and dignity.* Leaves.

ROSAURA: *Alas, what is this chill running through my veins? What commotion storms my heart!* (To THE PROMPTER.) Speak softly, I know this part. *Will Florindo ever return to my house now that he has been discovered by his father? Will he ever be mine to wed? Oh, grief smites me! Oh, what sorrow . . .* Speak up, I don't remember this part. *Oh, what sorrow overwhelms me! Unhappy Rosaura, will you be able to live without your beloved Florindo? How will you bear this painful . . .* Hush! *this painful separation? No. At the cost of losing all, at the cost of peril and death, I must go seek my idol, I must overcome this adverse . . . this adverse . . . fate . . . and let the world know . . .* Oh, damn this prompter! You can't hear him. I refuse to say another word. *Leaves.*

Scene VII

Enter PROMPTER *with book in hand, then* VITTORIA.

PROMPTER: Come on, *Colombina.* It's *Colombina's* turn and then *Harlequin's.* This cursed job! There's no end to it! You have to stay here three or four hours, shouting your lungs out, only to have the actors scold you and complain. It has already struck two,[21] and Heaven knows if the director will even ask me to dine with him. *(Calls loudly.) Colombina!*

VITTORIA: Yes, here I am.

PROMPTER: Let's begin, it's late. *(Withdraws and starts to prompt.)*

COLOMBINA: *Poor Rosaura, my poor mistress! Whatever makes her weep and despair so? Ah, I know what medicine she needs. A nice hot-blooded man will make her melancholy pass. But the trouble is that I need the same medicine my-self. Brighella and Harlequin are both blind with love over me and I don't know which I should prefer. Brighella is too clever, Harlequin too foolish. The clever one will want to do everything his way, while the foolish one won't know how to do anything my way; Brighella will plague me by day, Harlequin by night. If only someone would tell me what to do.*

Scene VIII

Enter BRIGHELLA (ANSELMO) *and* HARLEQUIN[22] (GIANNI), *who both overhear.*

---

[21] Literally, twenty, since the hours in Goldoni's plays are counted from six in the evening.

[22] Brighella and Harlequin speak Venetian.

COLOMBINA: *I know what I'll do. I'll go about town and every woman I meet I'll ask whether it's better to marry a shrewd man or a simple man.*

BRIGHELLA: (Comes forth.) *Shrewd, shrewd.*

HARLEQUIN: (Comes forth.) *Simple, simple.*

COLOMBINA: *Each for his own cause.*

BRIGHELLA: *I tell you the truth.*

HARLEQUIN: *And I tell you no lies.*

BRIGHELLA: *I'll prove it to you with all my gray matter.*

HARLEQUIN: *And I'll prove it to you with all my green matter.*

COLOMBINA: *Fine, and whoever persuades me will be my husband.*

BRIGHELLA: *Since I'm a shrewd man I'll toil and sweat so you'll always have plenty to eat.*

COLOMBINA: *That's a good point.*

HARLEQUIN: *Since I'm a simple man who doesn't know how to do anything, I'll let our friends bring us food and drink.*

COLOMBINA: *This way, too, would suit me.*

BRIGHELLA: *Since I'm a shrewd man who knows how to maintain honor, I'll make everyone respect you.*

COLOMBINA: *Good.*

HARLEQUIN: *Since I am an ignorant and peace-loving man, I'll see that everybody loves you.*

COLOMBINA: *That I wouldn't mind at all.*

BRIGHELLA: *Since I am a shrewd man, I'll run the house to perfection.*

COLOMBINA: *Fine.*

HARLEQUIN: *And since I am a simple man, I'll let you run it yourself.*

COLOMBINA: *Better.*

BRIGHELLA: *If you want distraction I'll escort you wherever you like.*

COLOMBINA: *Very good.*

HARLEQUIN: *If you want distraction I'll let you go alone wherever you like.*

COLOMBINA: *Excellent.*

BRIGHELLA: *If I catch some fop insulting you I'll see that he never forgets it.*

COLOMBINA: *Good.*

HARLEQUIN: *If I find anyone following you about I'll let chance take care of him.*

COLOMBINA: *Wonderful.*

BRIGHELLA: *If I find a prowler in our house I'll break his neck.*

HARLEQUIN: *And I'll hold the candle to give him light.*

BRIGHELLA: *Well, what do you say?*

HARLEQUIN: *Well, what do you think?*

COLOMBINA: *Now that I've heard all your arguments I conclude that Brighella is too strict and Harlequin is too patient. Therefore, do the following: knead yourselves together and make of two mad men one sage. Then I shall marry you.*

Leaves.

BRIGHELLA: *Harlequin?*

HARLEQUIN: *Brighella?*

BRIGHELLA: *What shall we do?*

HARLEQUIN: *What shall we do?*

BRIGHELLA: *Since your face is so pasty why don't you knead it into a dish of noodles?*

HARLEQUIN: *And since your noodle is so tasty why don't you serve it up with tomato sauce?*

BRIGHELLA: *Enough of this. It's beneath my dignity to compete with someone like you.*

HARLEQUIN: *You know what we can do? Colombina, when she likes, can be sly and cautious: so let's knead the two of us with her, and out of our three doughs we'll have a biscuit good enough for galley slaves.* Leaves.

Scene IX

BRIGHELLA, *then* ORAZIO *and* EUGENIO.

BRIGHELLA: *I see that this fellow is a clever fool; still it won't be honorable to let him outdo me. This calls for wit and ingenuity. As the pilot who finds himself on the high seas observes from the needle of his compass that the wind shifts from nor'easter to sou'wester, and orders his mariners to turn the sails, likewise I, to the mariners of my thoughts . . .*

ORAZIO: That's enough, that's enough!

ANSELMO: By your grace, sir, why don't you want me to finish my scene?

ORAZIO: Because these comparisons, these allegories, are no longer used.

ANSELMO: But whenever we use them the audience claps.

ORAZIO: Yes, but look who it is who claps. Educated people will never put up with such word play. What beastly nonsense! Comparing a man in love to a pilot at sea and then saying *the mariners of my thoughts!* The playwright simply never wrote these things. You pulled this simile out of your own head.

ANSELMO: So I shouldn't use parallels at all?

ORAZIO: No sir, no.

ANSELMO: And I shouldn't try to make up allegories?

ORAZIO: No, again no.

ANSELMO: So I should think more with my brains and less with my tongue.   *Leaves.*

Scene X

ORAZIO *and* EUGENIO.

ORAZIO: You see? This is exactly why actors should never

stray from the written text. They fall too easily into what is old-fashioned and implausible.

EUGENIO: Then do you think we should do away with improvised comedies altogether?

ORAZIO: Altogether, no. In fact it's a good thing that Italians continue to do what other countries have never dared. The French say that Italian actors are rash for improvising before the public, but what may be considered rashness in an ignorant comedian is a virtue in a skilled one. We have some excellent actors in Italy who do our country and our profession great honor, and they achieve no less elegance through their admirable art of improvisation than a poet can achieve through writing.

EUGENIO: But our masked characters usually find it very difficult to act when their roles have been written out.

ORAZIO: Ah, but when a masked character is given a role that has been written with charm and wit and is well suited to his nature, then you can be sure that if he is worth his salt he will gladly memorize the part.

EUGENIO: Couldn't we do away with masks in our comedies?

ORAZIO: Heaven help us if we ever made such an innovation. The time is not ripe yet. In all things one should never try to go against the universal consensus. At one time people used to go to the theatre just to laugh; they wanted to see nothing but masks on stage, and whenever a serious character came out to recite a dialogue that was a little too long, they immediately grew bored. Now they're beginning to enjoy the serious roles, too; they like the dialogues and delight in unexpected turns in the plot, they appreciate the moral and laugh at the quips and sallies contained in the serious scenes. But they also enjoy the masked characters, and we shouldn't eliminate them altogether. In fact, we should try instead to place them properly and to support them in all their ridiculousness, even next to the most clever and graceful of serious characters.

EUGENIO: But to compose comedies in such a way is extremely difficult.

ORAZIO: It's a way of writing that was rediscovered only recently and charmed everyone at its first appearance; it won't be long before the most inventive minds will be aroused to improve it, as its originator desires with all his heart.

Scene XI

Enter PETRONIO.

PETRONIO: Your servant, gentlemen.

ORAZIO: My respects to you, Petronio.

PETRONIO: I wanted to rehearse my scenes, too, but it seems no one is very willing to hear me.

ORAZIO: We'll stop here this morning and after dinner we'll continue rehearsing.

PETRONIO: But I live far from here and wouldn't want to walk all the way home and back again.

EUGENIO: Oh, then you can stay and dine with Orazio. I'm already counting on eating here myself.

ORAZIO: Why you are most welcome, my patrons!

Scene XII

Enter PROMPTER, *then* ANSELMO *and* LELIO.

PROMPTER: *(From within to* ORAZIO.*)* If that is the case, then I too shall stay and partake of your hospitality.

ORAZIO: *(As* PROMPTER *enters.)* Sir, I'm astonished that you hesitate.

ANSELMO: Orazio, you've always been so well inclined toward me that I'm sure you won't refuse me a favor this time.

LELIO   *bows.*

ORAZIO: Please tell me and I'll do my best to serve you . . .

LELIO   *bows.*

ANSELMO: Lelio is here and he wishes to become an actor. He has some wit and skill, and our company needs another *amoroso.* For my sake, will you be so kind as to accept him?

LELIO   *bows.*

ORAZIO: To content you, my dear Anselmo, I would accept him with pleasure. Only how can I be assured that he knows how to act?

ANSELMO: Well, why don't we try him out? Lelio, are you willing to give us an audition?

LELIO: I'd be most happy to, but I'm terribly sorry that right now I can't. I haven't had my chocolate this morning and my voice and stomach are rather weak.

ORAZIO: Look, why don't we come back after eating and rehearse then?

LELIO: But in the meantime where am I to go?

ORAZIO: Why, go home and then return.

LELIO: But I have no home.

ORAZIO: Then where are you staying?

LELIO: I'm not staying anywhere.

ORAZIO: How long have you been in Venice?

LELIO: Since yesterday.

ORAZIO: And where did you eat yesterday?

LELIO: I ate nowhere yesterday.

ORAZIO: You ate nothing at all?

LELIO: Neither yesterday nor this morning.

ORAZIO: Then what do you plan to do?

EUGENIO: My dear poet, come to the director's for dinner.

LELIO: I shall accept your hospitality, Signor Director, for these are the adversities in the life of a poet.

ORAZIO: I'll receive you not as a poet, but as an actor.

PETRONIO: Come along, Lelio, come along. Actors have these adversities, too, when it comes to rehearsals.

ORAZIO: Oh, I beg your pardon! At this rate I'll run up a fine bill!

LELIO: Well, that's settled, so let us speak no more of it. Today you will see my ability.

PETRONIO: And we shall soon see you demonstrate it at the dinner table.

Scene XIII

Enter VITTORIA.

VITTORIA: Signor Orazio, there's a foreign lady at the door, all covered with little curls, very perky, with a little cloak and a little hat, and she wants to see the head of the company.

ORAZIO: Let her come up.

LELIO: Wouldn't it be better to receive her after dinner?

ORAZIO: No, let's see what she wants.

VITTORIA: We'll show her in then.

ORAZIO: No, let's send a servant.

VITTORIA: I'll go myself. If a servant I am on stage, then a servant I can be in life.

Scene XIV

Enter PLACIDA *and* BEATRICE.

PLACIDA: What pomp! What pomp!
BEATRICE: What beauty! What beauty!
ORAZIO: What is it, my ladies?
PLACIDA: An enchanting foreign lady coming up the stairs.
BEATRICE: She even has a footman in livery. She must be a grand lady indeed!
ORAZIO: We'll soon see; here she is!

Scene XV

Enter ELEONORA *with* FOOTMAN.

ELEONORA: Ladies and gentlemen, your servant.
ORAZIO: Your most humble servant, milady. *(The ladies curtsey to her and all the men take off their hats.)*
ELEONORA: Pray tell me, are you actors?
ORAZIO: Yes, madam, at your service.
ELEONORA: Which of you is the head of the company?
ORAZIO: I am, at your service.
ELEONORA: *(Toward* PLACIDA.*)* And are you possibly the leading lady?
PLACIDA: *(With a curtsey.)* At your command.
ELEONORA: Good. I know you do yourself honor.
PLACIDA: Thank you for your generosity.
ELEONORA: I too take pleasure in going to comedies, and when I see buffoonery I split with laughter.
ORAZIO: So as not to fail in my duty, pray tell me, with whom do we have the honor of speaking?

ELEONORA: I am a virtuoso in music. *(All look at one another and put their hats back on.)*

ORAZIO: You are a singer, then?

ELEONORA: I am a virtuoso in music.

ORAZIO: Do you perhaps teach music?

ELEONORA: No, sir, I sing.

ORAZIO: Therefore you are a singer.

PLACIDA: *(To* ELEONORA.*)* Do you play the leading lady?

ELEONORA: Sometimes I do.

PLACIDA: *(Mocking her.)* Good. I shall come to see you.

PETRONIO: I too, madam, when I hear singers whining away, I too split with laughter.

LELIO: Forgive me if your ladyship will be so kind, but are you not Signora Eleonora?

ELEONORA: Yes sir, I am indeed.

LELIO: Don't you recall that once you acted in one of my dramas?

ELEONORA: Where? I cannot remember.

LELIO: In Florence.

ELEONORA: What was the drama called?

LELIO: *Harlequin Dido.*[23]

ELEONORA: Yes sir, it's true. I played the leading role. In fact, the impresario was ruined because of the script.

LELIO: Everyone said it was because of the leading lady, but let that pass.

BEATRICE: Then you act in comic operas?

ELEONORA: Yes, madam, at times.

BEATRICE: And still you come to laugh at the buffooneries of players?

[23] Literally, *Dido in the Style of Berni.* Francesco Berni (1497–1535) gave his name to the whimsical, burlesque style of his humorous verse.

ELEONORA: Let me tell you. I like your way of doing things so much that it would give me great pleasure to join your company.

ORAZIO: You wish to become an actress?

ELEONORA: What? Me, an actress?

ORAZIO: Then what do you want of us?

ELEONORA: I'll come to sing the intermezzos.

ORAZIO: I am most obliged for your generosity.

ELEONORA: I shall find my own partner, and with one hundred *zecchini* you will cover both our expenses.

ORAZIO: Only one hundred *zecchini*?

ELEONORA: Plus travel, lodging, a small wardrobe; these things, of course, we can arrange later.

ORAZIO: Why of course, that is quite customary.

ELEONORA: We have our own intermezzos, and we'll do four at each performance, as covered by the fee; should you request more, you will pay us ten *zecchini* for each additional one.

ORAZIO: That too sounds very fair.

ELEONORA: And then, of course, there must be an adequate orchestra.

ORAZIO: That is understood.

ELEONORA: New attire.

ORAZIO: I have a tailor in the house.

ELEONORA: My footman fills the mute parts and will be satisfied with whatever you offer him.

ORAZIO: I see your servant is equally modest.

ELEONORA: Then it seems to me the affair is settled.

ORAZIO: Quite settled.

ELEONORA: So . . .

ORAZIO: So, madam, we have no need for you.

ALL: *(Delighted.)* Bravo! Bravo!

ELEONORA: What! You disdain me so?

ORAZIO: Madam, do you believe that actors have to rely on music for their success? Unfortunately, for some time our profession has been so debased as to coax people to the theatre with music. But thank Heaven everyone has seen the light. I don't wish to discuss the merits or faults of singing maestros, but I will say that when both know their professions, the actor is just as worthy as the musician; with this difference, however, that in order to appear before the public, we must study; you, on the other hand, simply mouth a couple of arias like parrots, and then, by relying on your claque, have yourselves applauded. Signora Virtuoso, your humble servant.

Leaves.

ELEONORA: Just as usual: actors are always enemies of virtuosos.

PLACIDA: No, madam, that's not so. Actors respect musicians who have merit and ability; but musicians and virtuosos, if they have any merit, also respect honorable and upright actors. If you were a celebrated virtuoso you would never have come here offering yourself for theatre intermezzos. However, if you succeed you will certainly improve your condition, since it is far better to live among ordinary actors like ourselves than among the bad musicians with whom you have obviously associated until now. Signora Virtuoso, I bid you good day.   *Leaves.*

ELEONORA: Why, this lady must have once played the princess and never recovered.

BEATRICE: Like yourself, madam. You once saw some sheets of music and were convinced you were a true virtuoso. The time has passed when the comic stage was the slave of music. Now our theatre is filled with nobility, and if once they came to you to admire, and to us to laugh, now they come to us to enjoy comedies and to you to make conversation. *Leaves.*

ELEONORA: These actors are bold indeed. Gentlemen, I had never expected such treatment from you.

EUGENIO: You would have been treated much better had you come with better manners.

ELEONORA: But we virtuosos all speak this way.

EUGENIO: And we actors all answer this way. *Leaves.*

ELEONORA: Curse the moment I ever set foot in here!

PETRONIO: Indeed you have made a mistake to come here and dirty your virtuoso's shoes on an actor's stage . . .

ELEONORA: And pray tell, who are you?

PETRONIO: The Doctor, to serve you.

ELEONORA: The Doctor in the comedy?

PETRONIO: Just as you are a virtuoso in the theatre.

ELEONORA: Hence you are a doctor without doctrine.

PETRONIO: Hence you are a virtuoso without knowing how to read or write. *Leaves.*

ELEONORA: This is too much. If I stay here my reputation will be ruined. Footman, I wish to leave.

ANSELMO: Signora Virtuoso, if you care to remain here and eat rice with the actors, you are welcome.

ELEONORA: Oh, you are a most proper and civil gentleman.

ANSELMO: I'm not the master of the house, but the head of the company is such a good friend of mine that if I took you to him, I'm sure he'd receive you with pleasure.

ELEONORA: But I'll lose all respect before the women.

ANSELMO: Simply act with a little prudence and you'll see how kindly they'll treat you.

ELEONORA: Then go tell the head of the company, and if he invites me, I might be induced to come.

ANSELMO: I'll go immediately. *(Aside.)* (Now I understand. This lady's music keeps company with Signor Lelio's poetry. Their hunger is enough to make your skin crawl!)
Leaves.

LELIO: Signora Eleonora, since we have known each other for some time, you can speak to me frankly. Tell me, how are things going for you?

ELEONORA: Quite badly. The impresario of the opera in which I sang went bankrupt; I lost my pay and had to travel at my own expense; and to tell you the truth, I have nothing but what you see about me.

LELIO: Madam, I am in much the same condition, but if you care to follow the same road I have chosen, you too will be better off.

ELEONORA: And what have you decided to do?

LELIO: To become an actor.

ELEONORA: And must I degrade myself so?

LELIO: My dear lady, how is your appetite?

ELEONORA: Rather good.

LELIO: And mine is excellent. Let us go dine and discuss the matter later.

ELEONORA: But the head of the company hasn't sent me his invitation.

LELIO: Don't worry. Come along. He's a gentleman and won't refuse you.

ELEONORA: I don't find it very easy.

LELIO: Well, if you don't find it easy, I do. I'm off to hear the harmony of spoons, which is the most beautiful music in the world.   *Leaves.*

ELEONORA: Well, footman, what shall we do?

FOOTMAN: I'm so hungry I can hardly stand up.

ELEONORA: Should we go, or shouldn't we?

FOOTMAN: For the love of God, let's go!

ELEONORA: But how will I ever overcome my embarrassment? What should I do? Should I be persuaded to become an actress? I'll go eat with the actors and . . . yes, that decides it. Then, finally, it's all theatre, and from a bad musician I might become a fairly good actress. Just think how my companions would jump at such a chance! It's much better to earn your bread by hard work than to give people a chance to gossip.   *Leaves with* FOOTMAN.

Act Three

Scene I

ORAZIO *and* EUGENIO.

EUGENIO: Now the company is truly complete. Signor Lelio and Signora Eleonora will fill the two parts we needed.

ORAZIO: But who knows if they know how to act?

EUGENIO: You can always try them out, but I think they'll do very well.

ORAZIO: And then we'll have to see how they deport themselves. One has poetry in his head, the other has music; I wouldn't want them to irritate me with their opinions. As you know, in my company I value peace above all, and I have more respect for a player who has good manners than for a fine actor who is vexatious and troublesome.

EUGENIO: And so it should be. Harmony among colleagues makes for the success of plays. Where there are dissension and envy and jealousy, everything goes badly.

ORAZIO: I can't understand what made Signora Eleonora decide to become an actress so suddenly.

EUGENIO: Why, necessity has driven her to procure this bit of bread.

ORAZIO: And as soon as her situation has improved she'll do just as so many others; she'll forget our kindness and turn her back on us.

EUGENIO: Well, that is the way the world has always been.

ORAZIO: Ingratitude is a great fault.

59

EUGENIO: Yet there are many who are ungrateful.

ORAZIO: Look. Signor Lelio is getting ready to recite something for his audition.

EUGENIO: He'll soon be over here, and I wouldn't want to intimidate him.

ORAZIO: Yes, you're right, you'd better leave. Go to Signora Eleonora, and when I've finished with the poet send me the virtuoso.

EUGENIO: The uncouth poet and the ludicrous virtuoso, a fine pair!   *Leaves.*

Scene II

ORAZIO, *then* LELIO.

ORAZIO: Here he comes now and with such a solemn tread. He's no doubt going to put on quite a scene!

LELIO: *I have been to see my beloved, and having had no fortune in finding her at home, I wish to bring myself to the market to seek her there.*

ORAZIO: Signor Lelio, to whom do you think you are speaking?

LELIO: But can't you see I'm acting?

ORAZIO: Yes, I understand you're acting, but while you are acting, to whom are you speaking?

LELIO: To myself. I'm making my entrance; this is a soliloquy.

ORAZIO: And when speaking to yourself do you say, *I have been to see my beloved?* A man all by himself doesn't speak this way. Instead it seems as if you have come on stage to tell someone where you have been.

LELIO: Very well, then, I was speaking to the audience.

ORAZIO: Just as I expected. Don't you understand that one

simply cannot speak to the audience? When an actor's alone on the stage he must suppose that he is neither heard nor seen. Addressing the audience is an insufferable habit, and should never be permitted.

LELIO: But this is the way nearly all actors improvise. When they come on stage alone nearly all actors begin to tell the audience where they've been or where they intend to go, so shouldn't we do the same?

ORAZIO: No, because they're wrong, very wrong.

LELIO: Then shouldn't we ever make soliloquies?

ORAZIO: Why, certainly you should. Soliloquies are necessary to express one's innermost feelings, to inform the audience of a person's character and to show the effects and changes of the passions.

LELIO: But how is one to make a soliloquy without speaking to the audience?

ORAZIO: Nothing could be simpler. Listen to this speech of yours when it is more natural and normal. Rather than saying, *I have been to my beloved's house and found her not; I wish to go and seek her*, say it this way: *Unhappy chance, since you have denied me the joy of finding my beloved at home, allow me to find her . . .*

LELIO: At the market.

ORAZIO: Oh, this is even more elegant! Do you want to meet your beloved at the market?

LELIO: Yes sir, at the market. I was imagining that my beloved was a vendor, and if you had permitted me to finish, you would have found out from my speech who I am, who she is, how we fell in love, and how I intend to carry out our courtship.

ORAZIO: All these things you want to say by yourself? Keep in mind that the argument of a play should never be presented by only one person, for it is implausible that a man, speaking alone, would tell himself the story of his loves and misfortunes. In the past our players used to introduce the argument in the first scene, either through Pantalone speaking to the Doctor, or a master speaking to his servant, or a mistress to her maid. But the right way to present the situation without boring the audience is to divide it into several scenes, and little by little reveal it, to the pleasure and surprise of the listeners.

LELIO: Good gracious, Signor Orazio, these improvised plays are not for me! Your rules are unusual, and since I've just begun to act I'll never keep up with the others. Let me act in memorized plays instead.

ORAZIO: Very well, but you must remember that you'll need time to learn a part, and it will be a while before I'll be able to hear you.

LELIO: I'll act something of my own for you.

ORAZIO: Excellent. Speak up, I'm listening.

LELIO: I'll recite a piece from a comedy in verse.[24]

ORAZIO: Go ahead. But tell me in all confidence, are these lines your own?

LELIO: Well, I'm afraid not.

ORAZIO: Then whose are they?

LELIO: I'll tell you later. In this scene a father is trying to persuade his daughter not to marry.

---

[24] Earlier editions of the play included the following dialogue:

ORAZIO: In verse? That's a pity.

LELIO: But good Italian comedies ought to be in verse. That is the way ancient comedies were written, and some moderns feel that is the way they should be written.

ORAZIO: I revere the ancients and respect the moderns, but I am not convinced. Comedy must be wholly plausible, and it is not plausible that people should speak in verse. Oh, you will tell me the verse need not be recognized as such, and should sound like prose. But if that is so, then write in prose.

LELIO: Don't you want me to recite these verses?

Oh Daughter, you are dearer to me than
Ever I could say, and know the things
I've done for you; before you choose the iron
Fetters of matrimony, hear the woes
That follow on the conjugal embrace.
Beauty and youth, the precious gifts of woman,
Are soon by marriage crushed and put to flight!
And then before you're ready children come!
And what a hardship to bear in the womb,
Give birth, and bring them up and nourish them:
These are the things that make your blood run cold!
And who's to say your husband won't be jealous,
Forbidding you the things he seeks himself?
Think, Daughter, think; and after you have thought
Better of it, then I will stand by you,
A father to console you as I'm now
A father to advise you.

ORAZIO: You know, that doesn't really sound like verse.

LELIO: Do you want to hear it as verse? Listen to how one can make these lines sound like verse if one wishes. *(He recites the same lines, declaiming them to bring out the meter.)*

ORAZIO: True. It is verse, and yet it didn't seem so. Tell me, my friend, who wrote these lines?

LELIO: You ought to know.

ORAZIO: Yet I don't.

LELIO: They are by the author of your plays.

ORAZIO: But how is this possible if up to now he has never written in verse?

LELIO: Actually, he didn't want to write them, but to me, a fellow poet, he has confided this scene.

ORAZIO: Then you know him?

LELIO: Yes, I know him and hope some day to be able to compose comedies as he does.

ORAZIO: Well, my boy, before you can hope to accomplish anything you must devote as many years to the theatre as he has. Do you think he learned to write comedies overnight? He worked at it little by little, and only after long study, long practice and a continual and tireless observation of the theatre, of people's customs, and of the spirit of different countries, did he become a successful playwright.

LELIO: Tell me something. Is my acting good enough?

ORAZIO: It will do.

LELIO: Then will you accept me in your company?

ORAZIO: Yes, with pleasure.

LELIO: Then I am very happy. I will devote myself to acting and renounce my fancy for writing. Dear me! There are as many rules for writing a play as there are words that go to make it up. *Leaves.*

Scene III

ORAZIO, *and then* ELEONORA.

ORAZIO: This young fellow has spirit. Seems a bit footloose,[25] as the Florentines say; but in the theatre there is always need for someone who can play the livelier roles.

ELEONORA: Your servant, Signor Orazio.

ORAZIO: My respects to Signora Virtuoso.

ELEONORA: Please don't humiliate me any more. I realize I introduced myself to you with little grace and that I

[25] *Girellaio.* Florentine speech shows a predilection for the suffix *-aio.*

needed rescuing: it's my musical background that's to blame. But the affability, the propriety and modesty of your women have made me fall in love with them and with all of you. This clearly disproves the belief that women of the theatre are morally lax and supplement their incomes from the stage by practicing an older profession at home.

ORAZIO: I'm happy to be able to say that not only have immoral practices been done away with among theatre people, but the plays themselves have been purged of scandal. No longer does one hear obscene words, dirty equivocations, or unchaste dialogues. No longer does one find risqué jokes, improper gestures, or lewd scenes that set a bad example. Now young ladies can go to the theatre without fear of learning anything immodest or insidious.

ELEONORA: Well, sir, I want to become an actress, and I am relying on you to see me through.

ORAZIO: Oh, but you should rely on yourself. You must study, observe other actors, learn your parts well, and above all, if you hear a little applause, don't let it go to your head, don't suddenly put on the airs of a great lady. If you hear clapping, distrust it. Applause is usually misleading. Many clap from habit, others from passion, some merely by temperament, others out of personal interest, and many, many others because they are paid by protectors . . .

ELEONORA: But I have no protectors.

ORAZIO: You were a singer and have no protectors?

ELEONORA: I have none, and I am placing myself entirely in your hands.

ORAZIO: But I am the head of the company. I love everybody equally and I want everyone to do well for his own sake as well as mine; I can't favor anyone, especially not a woman, because however good women may be, they always envy one another.

ELEONORA: But won't you even give me an audition? Won't you try me in that role of third lady you offered me?

ORAZIO: Oh yes, certainly. It's in my interest to be sure you can act well.

ELEONORA: I'll try some *recitativi* I know.

ORAZIO: But not to music.

ELEONORA: I'll do it without music. This is a scene from Signor Lelio's *Harlequin Dido*.

ORAZIO: The play that ruined your impresario?

ELEONORA: Just listen: *(Turns toward* ORAZIO *to recite.)*
   Aeneas, splendor of Asia . . .

ORAZIO: I beg your pardon, madam, but would you kindly turn your waist toward the audience . . .

ELEONORA: But if I must speak to Aeneas . . .

ORAZIO: Well, you should stand facing the audience, then gracefully turn your head slightly toward the other character. Watch:
   Aeneas, splendor of Asia . . .

ELEONORA: But that's not the way my voice maestros taught me.

ORAZIO: Yes, I know all too well. You people pay attention to nothing but the cadence.

ELEONORA:
   Aeneas, splendor of Asia,
   Cherished son of Venus
   And only love of these so tender lights;
   Look how in Carthage, joyful as a child
   By your return consoled,
   Even the towers dance the gay Furlana.[26]

[26] A violent Venetian dance.

ORAZIO: Enough, enough, for Heaven's sake, please say no more!

ELEONORA: Why not? Do I act so badly?

ORAZIO: No, your acting is all right, but I cannot bear to hear these exquisite and graceful lines of *Dido* made ridiculous; and had I known that Lelio mistreated the dramas of so celebrated and venerable a poet,[27] I would never have accepted him in my company; he will not dare to do it again, I'll see to it. We owe too much to this poet and have never ceased to benefit from his works.

ELEONORA: Do you believe, then, that I am acceptable as an actress?

ORAZIO: As a beginner you are acceptable; your voice is not firm, but you will acquire that with acting. Be careful to stress the final syllables so they can be understood. Speak slowly, but not excessively so, and in the emotional parts build up your voice and accelerate the words more than usual. Be careful, above all, not to fall into sing-song or declamation, but utter your words naturally as if you were speaking. Drama is an imitation of nature, and in it one should do only what is plausible. And as for gestures, they too should be natural. Move your hands according to the sense of the words. Make your gestures mostly with the right hand and seldom with the left, and avoid moving them both at once, unless an impulse of rage, or surprise, or an exclamation requires it; and remember the rule that if you begin a sentence with one hand, you should finish it with that same hand and not the other. I must also warn you of something else which is much

[27] Metastasio's *Dido abandonata* and *Cato in Utica* are burlesqued here by Lelio.

seen but little understood. When another character is on stage with you, pay attention to him, and don't let your eyes or mind wander; don't gaze here and there among the sets or into the boxes, because there will be three dreadful consequences. The first is that the audience grows indignant and believes that the character is either ignorant or distracted. Secondly, you offend your partner; and finally, when your attention strays from the sense of the dialogue, the prompter's words come unexpectedly, making you act awkwardly and unnaturally. All these things tend to ruin our profession and turn plays into disasters.

ELEONORA: I thank you for your advice and will try to put it into practice.

ORAZIO: When you have time free from acting, go to other theatres. Observe the work of good actors, since in this profession one learns more through the art itself than through rules about it.

ELEONORA: That, too, sounds wise.

ORAZIO: Just a little warning and then we'll go so that the other players may continue rehearsing the rest of the comedy. Signora Eleonora, be friendly to all and familiar with none. If you hear someone speaking harmfully against your colleagues, try to say a word in their favor. If you hear something aimed against you, don't believe it, and ignore it. As for roles, take what is offered you; remember that it is the good part, not the large part, that brings an actor honor. Be diligent; come early to the theatre, try to be liked by all, and if a person seems ill-disposed towards you, use not flattery but dissimulation. Flattery is a vice, but wise dissimulation has always been a virtue.   *Leaves.*

ELEONORA: This director has given me some fine suggestions and I'm obliged to him. I'll do my best to make use of them; and since I've chosen to become an actress, if I can't be among the first, I'll do my best not to be the last. *Leaves.*

Scene IV

Enter PROMPTER, *then* PLACIDA *and* PETRONIO.

PROMPTER: Come, come, gentlemen, time is passing and it will soon be evening. Rosaura, Doctor, it's your turn.

DOCTOR: *Tell me, my daughter, what brings on this melancholy of yours? Is it possible that you don't want to confide in your loving father?*

ROSAURA: *In the name of Heaven, please do not torment me.*

DOCTOR: *Do you want a dress? I'll have one made for you. Do you want to go to the country? I'll take you. Do you want a ball? I'll arrange one. Do you want a husband? I'll . . .*

ROSAURA: (Sighing.) *Alas!*

DOCTOR: *Yes, I'll give you one. Tell me something, my sweet lass, are you in love?*

ROSAURA: (Crying.) *Oh Father, pity me in my weakness. Yes, unfortunately, I am in love.*

DOCTOR: *Come now, don't cry, I understand. You are at an age for marrying, and I won't fail to console you if he's a proper man. Tell me, who is this lover you are so pining for?*

ROSAURA: *The son of Signor Pantalone de' Bisognosi.*

DOCTOR: *The young man could not be better. I'm delighted. If he desires you, then you shall have him.*

ROSAURA: (Catching her breath.) *Ah!*

DOCTOR: *Yes, you shall have him, you shall have him.*

Scene V

Enter COLOMBINA.

COLOMBINA: *The poor thing! I haven't the heart to watch him suffer so.*

DOCTOR: *What is it, Colombina?*

COLOMBINA: *There's a poor lad who walks under the windows of this house, and he cries, and he's desperate, and he knocks his head against the wall.*

ROSAURA: *Oh dear! Who is it? Tell me!*

COLOMBINA: *It's that poor Signor Florindo.*

ROSAURA: *My love, my heart, my soul. Father, for the love of Heaven!*

DOCTOR: *Yes, my dear daughter, I want to make you happy. Hurry, Colombina, call him and say that I wish to speak to him.*

COLOMBINA: *I won't waste a moment; oh, when it comes to serving young people I'm all joy.*   Leaves.

ROSAURA: *Oh, Father dear, you do love me so!*

DOCTOR: *Why, you are the sole fruit of my love.*

ROSAURA: *Will you give him to me as a husband?*

DOCTOR: *I will, I will.*

ROSAURA: *But there is one difficulty.*

DOCTOR: *What is it?*

ROSAURA: *Florindo's father will not be happy.*

DOCTOR: *Why not?*

ROSAURA: *Because the good man is in love with me too.*

DOCTOR: *Yes, I know, I know, but don't worry. We'll find a remedy for this too.*

Scene VI

Enter FLORINDO *and* COLOMBINA.

COLOMBINA: *Here he is, here he is! The relief is killing him!*

ROSAURA: (To herself.) *(Blessed be those eyes; I'm in a fever just looking at them!)*

FLORINDO: *Signor Doctor, please forgive me. Encouraged by Colombina . . . because if Signora Rosaura . . . Rather, her own father . . . Pray, have pity, I hardly know what I am saying.*

DOCTOR: *Now, now, I understand. You are in love with my daughter and you wish her hand. Is this not so?*

FLORINDO: *I could desire nothing better.*

DOCTOR: *But I hear that your father has some ridiculous intentions.*

FLORINDO: *My father is rival to his own son.*

DOCTOR: *Then we have no time to lose. We must destroy his hopes of ever obtaining her.*

FLORINDO: *But how?*

DOCTOR: *By immediately offering your hand to Rosaura.*

FLORINDO: *Oh, I'm so happy!*

ROSAURA: *Oh, I'm so comforted!*

COLOMBINA: *Oh, I'm so envious!*

DOCTOR: *Come then, let us conclude it. Join your hands.*

FLORINDO: *Here, with all my heart.*

ROSAURA: *Here, in witness to my faith.*
      (They join hands.)
COLOMBINA: *Oh, my dears! Oh, how lovely! I'm so happy my mouth is watering!*

Scene VII

Enter PANTALONE.

PANTALONE: *What goes on here? What sort of an affair is this?*

DOCTOR: *Signor Pantalone, though you haven't deigned to speak with me, I have nevertheless discovered your intentions and have blindly favored them.*

PANTALONE: *What do you mean? What intentions?*

DOCTOR: *Tell me, didn't you want my daughter to become Florindo's bride?*

PANTALONE: *Why no! By no means!*

DOCTOR: *But didn't you tell her you wanted her to marry into your family?*

PANTALONE: *Well yes, sir, but not to my son.*

DOCTOR: *To whom then?*

PANTALONE: *Why, to me, to me.*

DOCTOR: *I would never have guessed that at your age you had fallen to such folly. Pray, forgive me. I have misunderstood, and this misunderstanding has brought about the marriage of your son and my daughter, Rosaura.*

PANTALONE: *I'll never consent. It will never happen.*

DOCTOR: *On the contrary, it will indeed. If you do not consent I do. Both you and your son have made love to my daughter; hence one or the other must marry her. As far as I am concerned it can be either the father or the son. But since the son is the younger and the more swift-legged, he has arrived first; and you, who are old and couldn't finish, have had to quit when the race was half over.*

COLOMBINA: *Like all old people: after a few steps they have to stop and rest.*

PANTALONE: *I tell you, this is vile trickery. A father should not play his daughter's pander to trap the son of a gentleman, the son of a man of honor.*

FLORINDO: (TO PANTALONE.) *Come, Father, do not lose your temper.*

DOCTOR: *And a gentleman or a man of honor should not seduce the daughter of a good friend against the rules of hospitality and friendship.*

ROSAURA: (To the DOCTOR.) *Please, for the love of Heaven, don't quarrel!*

Scene VIII

Enter LELIO.

LELIO: Fine, my good players, fine. Oh, this is an excellent scene indeed. The director was telling me that the theatre has been reformed and that now all the good rules are observed; yet this scene of yours is a great blunder, it just won't do, it simply can't remain the way it is.

EUGENIO: And why won't it do? Just where is this blunder?

LELIO: It's one of the biggest and most outlandish blunders ever made.

TONINO: And who do you think you are, the head of the company himself?

VITTORIA: *(Makes the gesture of someone gorging himself.)* He is a very *faminous* poet.

PETRONIO: And he knows Virgil's *Bucklelegs* by heart.
LELIO: Well, there's one thing I do know for certain: this is
a bad scene.

Scene IX

Enter ORAZIO.

ORAZIO: What is this? Aren't we going to finish the rehearsal?
PLACIDA: We nearly finished, but then Lelio began scream-
ing and ranting that this scene was no good.
ORAZIO: What makes you say this, Lelio?
LELIO: I've been told that according to Horace's *Poetics* there
should never be more than three persons on stage at a
given time. In this scene there are five.
ORAZIO: I'm sorry, but you should tell whoever said this
that he is misinterpreting Horace. Horace said, *Nec
quarta loqui persona laboret.*[28] Some understand this to
mean that no more than three should work on stage at a
time. What he actually intended, though, was that if
there are four characters, the fourth should not be over-
worked; that is, the four actors should not get in each
other's way as happens in improvised scenes when four
or five persons are on stage and immediately create a
confusion. Otherwise, a scene can easily be made with
eight or ten persons, provided it is properly directed and
all the characters are made to speak in turn, without inter-
fering with one another. On this point all the best authors
agree when interpreting this passage from Horace.

[28] Literally, "Nor should the fourth character labor" (Horace,
Ars Poetica, 192). The passage is usually taken as implying that only
three speaking characters were to be on stage at a single time.

LELIO: Then I'm wrong here as well.

ORAZIO: Before speaking about the rules of the classical poets, one must consider two things: first, the true meaning of what they have written, and secondly, if what they have written is still valid for our own times; just as modes of dressing, eating, and conversing have changed, so have the tastes and rules of the theatre.

LELIO: And so tastes will continue to change, and the plays which you now praise will become old rags, like *The Statue, The False Prince,* and *Madam Pataffià.* [29]

ORAZIO: Plays will become old after they are put on over and over again; yet I would hope that the way of performing them will always bring new improvements. Characters that are credible and true to life will never lose their popularity, and though their number may be limited, the ways of interpreting them are not, because every virtue, every vice, every mannerism, every defect takes on different airs from different circumstances.

LELIO: There's one thing that will always be appreciated in the theatre.

ORAZIO: What's that?

LELIO: Criticism.

ORAZIO: Provided it is moderate; provided its object is not the particular but the universal, not the man but his vices; provided it remains criticism and does not fall into satire.

VITTORIA: My dear Orazio, with your good graces I must ask you either to let us finish the rehearsal or allow us to go home.

ORAZIO: You are perfectly right. This new actor is making

[29] *La statua, Il finto principe, Madama Pataffià.* Goldoni's note reads: *Among the worst of the* commedie dell' arte.

me set a bad precedent. *(To* LELIO.*)* Actors should never be interrupted when they are rehearsing.

LELIO: But I thought they had finished when Florindo and Rosaura were married. Everyone knows that comedies always end with marriages.

ORAZIO: No, not always.

LELIO: Then nearly always.

TONINO: Orazio, in this comedy I finish before the others; do you mind if I leave after I say my lines?

ORAZIO: No, do as you please.

Scene X

Enter PROMPTER.

PROMPTER: Oh, the devil! Are we going to finish this cursed play or not?

ORAZIO: Must you always yell? Whenever we rehearse you want to rush us through just for the sake of finishing early. During the performance if someone speaks in the wings you grumble so loudly everyone can hear you.

PROMPTER: Well, if I grumble I've good reason. This stage is always crowded with noisy spectators. I'm surprised at you for allowing so many of them to come here. We can hardly move.[30]

EUGENIO: I really can't understand what pleasure they find in coming on stage to see a play.

VITTORIA: Why, they do it to avoid sitting in the orchestra.

[30] In the earlier editions, Orazio says at this point: "This will not be true in the future. I must absolutely have the stage cleared." Goldoni included in his reform the banishment of spectators from the stage, as Garrick was doing at about the same time in England, and Voltaire in Paris.

EUGENIO: But it's much more enjoyable to watch a play from the orchestra than from the stage.

VITTORIA: Yes, but there are people who spit from the gallery and annoy those who are sitting below.

ORAZIO: True, we shall not have real order in our theatre until we learn this very simple rule of cleanliness.

EUGENIO: There's something else lacking and I'm afraid even to mention it.

ORAZIO: Speak out, we're the only ones here.

EUGENIO: They make a frightful clamor in the boxes.

ORAZIO: Yes, indeed, it's most trying.

PLACIDA: In all truth, it is extremely difficult for us players to act when the audience is making such an uproar. One must scream his lungs out to be heard, and still it's not enough.

VITTORIA: You simply have to be patient with the audience. What about the times you hear whistles and catcalls? Well, youth will be served. We simply must bear it.

ORAZIO: It's a pity they disturb the others.

PETRONIO: And when you hear them yawning?

ORAZIO: Then it means the play's a failure.

PETRONIO: But sometimes they do it out of malice, and mostly on opening nights, to ruin new comedies, if they are able.

LELIO: Do you know what people sing when they go to the theatre? A song from an intermezzo:

My man, no matter what you say,
I spent good money for this play,
And so I'm going to have my way.[31]

[31] These lines come from Metastasio's *L'Impresario delle Canarie*.

PROMPTER: Well, shall I go or not?

TONINO: Go on! Vanish! Begone!

PROMPTER: What way of speaking is this, Pantalone?

TONINO: Why with my mouth, Booby!

PROMPTER: I'm giving you fair warning, if you don't treat me with respect you'll be sorry. I'll have you speaking the worst blunders to the audience. If an actor is successful it's because of my good prompting. *Withdraws.*

ORAZIO: Our success, of course, depends on everyone's contribution.

PROMPTER: (Prompting within.) *I know that you are reluctant to have your son . . .* (Louder.) *I know that you are reluctant to have your son . . .*

TONINO: Go ahead, Doctor, it's your turn.

DOCTOR: All right, all right. *I know that you are reluctant to have your son marry, because you are in love with my daughter, but this weakness of yours wrongs both your character and your age. Rosaura would never have been persuaded to marry you; your love, therefore, was to no avail, and it is only just that you should satisfy your son. And if you love Rosaura you will perform a heroic deed; you will be an honest man, a sensible and prudent man, and yield to her the person who will make her happy, and in return you will be consoled by having been the cause of her true joy.*

PANTALONE: *Very well, I am a gentleman and a man of honor. I am very fond of the girl and I want to make an effort to show her my love. Florindo will wed your daughter, but since I've looked on her with no little passion and cannot forget her, I don't want to expose myself to the risk of having her in my own house, of living in perpetual hell. Florindo, may Heaven bless you, my son. Marry Rosaura, who deserves you, and live with her and her father as long as I am alive; I shall give you an honest and comfortable allowance. And you, my daughter-in-law, since you haven't loved* me, *go then and love my son. Treat him with tenderness and charity, and pity the weakness of a poor old man blinded more by your merits than by your beauty. My dear Doctor, come to my house and we shall make out the documents. If you have any requests, a little cash perhaps, here I am. I'll buy you what you want, I'll do anything, but this house I'll enter no more. Oh me! My heart is breaking. I can bear it no longer.* Leaves.

ROSAURA: *The poor man, I pity him so!*

Final Scene

Enter BRIGHELLA *and* HARLEQUIN.

HARLEQUIN: *Now, Colombina, to get back to our own proposition, come here and give me your hand.*

BRIGHELLA: *Ah, Colombina, could you be so cruel to Brighella?*

LELIO: There you are, Orazio, that's exactly how I ended my own play, and you didn't want to hear it. *(Pulls out some sheets and reads.) Florindo marries Rosaura. Harlequin marries Colombina, and the comedy ends with the two weddings.*

ORAZIO: You are indeed clever.

LELIO: And what is more . . .

GIANNI: Orazio, is there anything else to rehearse?

ORAZIO: No, that's all for now.

GIANNI: *(Removes his mask.)* You might have been kind enough to spare me all this work.

ORAZIO: Why?

GIANNI: Because I can do this sort of scene in my sleep.

ORAZIO: Now don't say that, my dear Harlequin. Don't say that. It takes a good actor to do even short scenes like this one, and when they are spoken and performed with grace they are doubly effective. And then, the shorter a scene is, the more it is liked. Though Harlequin must speak little, he must speak at the right moment. His lines must be recited effortlessly and with sparkle. Naturally, you will clip some words, but don't clip them all, and beware of those distortions which are so typical of a second Zanni. You must create something of your own, and to create you must study.

GIANNI: Pardon me, but it is possible to create without studying.

ORAZIO: How so?

GIANNI: Do as I have done: get married and have children.

Leaves.

ORAZIO: That was well put.

PLACIDA: If there's nothing more to rehearse, then I'll go, too.

ORAZIO: We're all leaving now.

EUGENIO: Yes, and we can stop at our director's for coffee.

ORAZIO: My masters, you are welcome a thousand times over.

LELIO: I want to ask you one last thing and that will be all.

ORAZIO: Please do.

LELIO: My play ended with a sonnet. I would like you to tell me whether it is correct to end a comedy with a sonnet.

ORAZIO: In some comedies sonnets are in keeping, while in others they are not. Our own author has sometimes used them properly, and other times he could have done without them. For example, *The Clever Woman* ends in an academy, so it is possible to close with a sonnet. In *The Honest Wench*, Bettina closes with a toast, which she does with a sonnet. In *The Good Wife* there is a final sonnet which describes how a good wife should act. In *The Cunning Widow* and *The Venetian Twins*[32] he could have left them out, and for the other plays he wrote no sonnets, because when there is no reason for them, they cannot and absolutely should not be written.

LELIO: Well, it's consoling to learn that even your poet makes mistakes.

ORAZIO: He's a man like any other, and is not beyond making errors. As a matter of fact, he himself has told me repeatedly that he trembles every time he must write a new play for this stage. He knows how difficult a problem it is, and he doesn't flatter himself into believing that he is able to compose the perfect comedy. But he is content to have given cultured and intelligent people the right encouragement so that some day the Italian theatre will recover the reputation it deserves.

PLACIDA: Orazio, I'm tired of standing here. Haven't you finished chattering yet?

ORAZIO: Come, let's go. The rehearsal is over. I think that from everything we've discussed and demonstrated today, you can see what, in our judgment, ought to be our Comic Theatre.

---

[32] *La donna di garbo, La putta onorata, La buona moglie, La vedova scaltra, I due gemelli veneziani.* The sonnets were in fact omitted from the two last plays when they were printed.

Appendix

Goldoni enjoyed a major triumph with the presentation of his comedy *The Cunning Widow* (*La vedova scaltra*) in 1748. As an example of plotted comedy lacking in romantic extravagances, it was recognized as initiating the reform of the theatre. The following season, in the autumn of 1749, the Brescian abbot Pietro Chiari presented an imitation and criticism of Goldoni's play, entitled *The School for Widows* (*La scuola delle vedove*). In reply, Goldoni wrote the following Prologue, which was published separately as an immediate defense of his play. In an attempt to put an end to the controversy, the Tribunal of the Inquisition banned further performances of both plays; and Chiari's version remained unpublished except for the *Argomento*, which included a list of the characters, as is noted in the text and notes below.

Goldoni had been given the name of Polisseno Fegejo on his initiation into the Arcadian Colony at Pisa (see his *Memoirs*, Chapter XVII). His interlocutor here is Girolamo Medebach, the Orazio of *The Comic Theatre*, whose name here may likewise suggest the prudence and temperance which Goldoni saw as the hallmarks of his theatrical reform.

D. C.

Apologetic Prologue to the Comedy entitled
THE CUNNING WIDOW
Against the criticisms contained in the Comedy entitled
The School for Widows

PRUDENZIO, *Reformer of the Theatres*
POLISSENO, *Poet*

PRUDENZIO: Master Polisseno, I hear you want to put your *Cunning Widow* on the stage again; it's full of defects and improprieties, so it ought to be corrected, if possible, before we can consider any new production.

POLISSENO: What, Master Prudenzio, now you come to me with this fine piece of news, after you've had a year to think about it? Should I have any hesitations about a new production of my *Cunning Widow*, when last year it appeared twenty-two evenings in Venice, when it was received repeatedly and with so much applause in Modena, in Bologna, in Parma, in Verona; when it was celebrated and performed by the very same people who now feel free to criticize it and slander it; after all this, I'm to correct it and repent at having written it? It won't be easy to persuade me of this, unless you can give me valid and conclusive reasons.

PRUDENZIO: The reasons must be quite well known to you without my bothering to repeat them. Have you seen *The School for Widows*?

POLISSENO: Yes indeed, sir, I have.

PRUDENZIO: What do you think of it? Is it a good comedy?

POLISSENO: Very good—when the audience applauds it.

PRUDENZIO: But what do you think of its criticisms of your *Cunning Widow*?

POLISSENO: To my mind its author has run true to form, just as if he had come to my dinner table, eaten his fill, and then insulted my food. *Facile inventis addere.* But to invent, to create: *Hoc opus, hic labor.*[1]

PRUDENZIO: This is all very true, and as for his inventiveness, we will come to that later. But one thing is certain anyway: he has touched you to the quick.

POLISSENO: At least he has tried to do so, notwithstanding all the fine claims he made in advance in the printed edition of his Argument, where he protested he had no intention of attacking any "recently produced" comedy; but it's not surprising that he should have failed to keep his word, for he had also proposed to give his Widow one character, and instead she appeared on stage with another.

PRUDENZIO: Let's leave that aside now; this is no time to discuss it.

POLISSENO: Yes, of course, we'll do it after he has published his fine Comedy.

PRUDENZIO: Come on now, defend yourself if you can. An Englishman, a Frenchman, and a Spaniard speak Italian perfectly: this is your first *Blunder.*[2]

POLISSENO: It would have been a blunder to have them speak differently. First of all, it is not unusual that Ultramontanes should speak Italian perfectly. I have dealt and conversed long and intimately with these people in Leghorn, in Genoa, and in Venice, and I assure you that some of them sound as if they had been born in Italy. In

---

[1] "It is easy to add to what has already been invented"; "This is the work, this is the task."

[2] Here and throughout this prologue Goldoni's use of italics marks allusions to details of *The School for Widows.*

my comedy I am not proposing three foreigners who
have arrived fresh from their countries and have sailed
their *Boat* up to the Inn—as if to imply they could
control the winds so as to arrive on the very day they
were expected by their friend.

PRUDENZIO: Now you're making criticism of criticism. My
dear Poets, if you continue this way, you will come to
bad ends.

POLISSENO: Believe me, I could give you tit for tat if I felt
so inclined. But let's go back to our subject. If I wanted
my three Ultramontanes to speak their own language
and stumble through ours badly, it wouldn't have been
difficult at all, because though I am not so well skilled
in English as I am in French, I could have asked a friend
to translate the Italian lines into English. But I didn't do
this, and I shouldn't have, for a number of reasons; the
first of them being that I would have had to find three
actors who could affect foreign tongues with some Italian
mixed in, as that Italian comedian who went by the name
of Monsieur della Petite used to do so brilliantly. You
can't say that a man speaks English just because he speaks
with his teeth clenched, and then uses only Italian words
in entirely Italian phrases. Nor is it enough, if you want to
convey that he's speaking English, to have some crazy
boatman pretend not to understand him, just to draw
laughter at the expense of a more serious character,
ridiculed in this fashion. An actor who mispronounces
ten or twelve French words and affects clumsily and
gracelessly to imitate the gestures of that nation can't be
said to play the role of a Frenchman; but rather (as the
celebrated Truffaldino[3] remarked extemporaneously) he

3 Goldoni refers here to the famous comedian Antonio Sacchi.

resembles a vendor of *Cattaro candles*.[4] If everyone spoke
as the Spaniard in *The School for Widows*, all would be
well, since that fine actor is skilled in Spanish, and not
only knows how to speak it, but also, at the right time
and in the right place, can make it intelligible by inserting
an Italian word or two. But that is to the credit of the
actor, not the author. It was this same actor who played
the Spaniard in my *Cunning Widow*; however, I begged
him to refrain from using any Spanish words, so as to
avoid a contrast with the other characters. Ah, Master
Prudenzio, *the language doesn't make the play*, the character does. The French present all their comedies in French.
In Paris, on the French stage, all the characters speak
French, no matter where they come from. Pantalone,
Harlequin, the Doctor all speak French, and the French
are just as convinced as I am that *the language doesn't
make the play*. *The Frenchman in London*,[5] which my
critic finds exemplary, has Frenchmen and Englishmen
alike speaking French; and in the Italian translation of
this play, presented by the Florentine Academicians, the
Frenchmen and Englishmen all speak Italian, and the
audience imagines they are speaking in their mother
tongues. Similarly in my play they must imagine that
everyone speaks in his own native tongue, translated
into Italian; and this is to aid the public's understanding,
so that the point of the character will not be lost as a
result of his broken speech, or undue ridicule cast on
other nationalities. Everyone likes to think he speaks
well; nobody enjoys hearing himself mocked, just as

[4] Another allusion, apparently, to *The School for Widows*.
[5] Louis de Boissy's *Le François à Londres* (1727; Florentine
version *ca.* 1744).

there is no Englishman who enjoys hearing a boatman call him *Panimbruo*. This word means *Heretic*: you just can't use that language on the stage. Besides, I had another reason for my Comedy which does not apply to *The School for Widows*. I introduce an English manservant and a French maidservant; now this girl is not merely there *to hold her hands on her hips like two handles on a pot*, but to convey sentiments peculiar to that country. If I had introduced foreign idioms, the Englishman would speak to his servant in a way that only a few would understand; and likewise, upon meeting the woman, the Frenchman would use his own language, and wouldn't be perfectly understood by everyone. But this fine Critic has seen the reef and has cleverly sailed around it; in fact he did even more: to avoid the necessity of having the Englishman and the other two foreigners speak their own tongues, he has had them arrive from Leghorn in a boat, and without a servant. Three gentlemen without a single servant? Why, they must be lower-class folk with little money, for noble and rich people would not make the sea voyage from Leghorn to Venice—which takes two months usually and often longer, to sail around the whole boot of Italy—when in five or six days one can go overland from Leghorn to Venice. The Critic has traveled little; the Critic has not even looked at the map.

PRUDENZIO: These reasons of yours do persuade me, and I hope they will persuade those who have good judgment. But there is a stronger objection yet, and I don't know how you will manage to defend yourself. You have your Widow disguise herself, you have her dress three times as a different foreigner, and you expect your Ultramontanes to take her as one of their compatriots, even though she is speaking Italian. Do you think her dress is enough to change her into a foreigner?

POLISSENO: I know myself that *it is not the hood that makes the monk*, but good actions and proper behavior. But I can easily defend myself against this criticism. You say that my Widow speaks Italian, and I say no. She speaks English, French, and Spanish, translated into Italian, just as the three foreigners were understood to speak; and the reasons I gave you for them apply to the Widow equally. What pleasure would the audience take in hearing this lady speak without understanding what she says? What distinguishes her in those three different disguises as a woman who is speaking translated languages is the phrasing which is conspicuously used more in one disguise than in another; thus the audience understands what she is saying, understands why she is taking the costume and manner of the various lands, and enjoys seeing her carry off so well her cunning device, and relishes the effects attained by her honest pranks. She is a clever woman, but an honest one, who is not teaching innocent girls how to entice men. She is no fool who disguises herself pointlessly, trying to approach foreigners in Cafés when she knows quite well her schemes will get her nowhere. This is indeed the case with the Widow of the *School*, who disguises herself solely to appear jolly and gay, while her masquerades contribute nothing to the plot of the comedy, since she makes us understand she does it on the advice of an intriguing servant and a demented sister-in-law.

PRUDENZIO: Let's not wander from the point, please. You are quite right: if the men can speak in translation, the same can be allowed for the woman. But how can you account

for her voice? How can you expect people to believe that
her four rival suitors don't recognize her by her voice?

POLISSENO: The mask alters the voice considerably.

PRUDENZIO: Haven't you heard exclamations here of
blunders, blunders?

POLISSENO: I can't recall: who said that?

PRUDENZIO: *Angelica.*

POLISSENO: *Angelica* said that, and she goes to the Café
herself, speaks with all four of them, and is not recognized by her voice? Not even the *Marchese Ottavio*
recognizes her, and he is her *cavalier servente?* Perhaps he
doesn't recognize her because she is speaking Venetian?
When it's not stated explicitly in the printed list of
characters,[6] you can't assume that Pantalone's daughter-
in-law is from out of town; hence Venetian is to be taken
as her native tongue. But the Poet makes her speak
Tuscan in his Comedy, and does the same with Pantalone's
own daughter, only for the sake of convention; and it is
for that same reason that my three foreigners in the
Cunning Widow speak Italian. What counts is that none
of them recognized her, and this shows that the mask
does alter a voice, and consequently I have committed
no *blunders,* and the criticism is unfounded.

PRUDENZIO: That is very fine, very fine indeed. You are to
be commended, I must say. But your trial is not over yet.
It is argued that you haven't studied your characters well,
and that you haven't portrayed them adequately.

---

[6] Chiari's published list of characters, though it is careful to note
the nationalities of foreign characters and even describes the Marchese
Ottavio as "*cavalier servente* of Angelica and of Italian nationality,"
lists Angelica and Isabella as simply "a young widow, the daughter-
in-law of Pantalone" and "the daughter of Pantalone," respectively.

POLISSENO: I shall answer like Corneille when he was criticized for his *Cid in Spain*. I appeal to the audience. Let
them judge, and I will submit to them. All I know is that
last year everyone in Venice spoke of nothing but their
admiration for the characters of *The Cunning Widow*, how
perfectly depicted they were, and how finely the players
did their job of interpreting the characters; and these
same players, albeit *cut-rate*,[7] are as good as any others,
and have brought tears to those who now think themselves unable to laugh. As for the Englishman, even the
author of the *School* characterizes him as a man of few
words, and then in the play itself he speaks much more
than all the others. As for the generosity of that country,
it is not in question; the manner and time of giving must
be taken into consideration according to needs and circumstances. My Englishman presumes to be preferred
over the others by the *Cunning Widow* and in order to
win her favor, gives her a ring which, during the ball,
she has praised highly and admired with enthusiasm. I
have presented a traveling Englishman, not a British
philosopher. As for the Frenchman, I don't know what
to say, except that the one in the *School* is not so clever
as mine. Mine, however, is not so fiery; the one in the
School has enough power all by himself to set a whole
household topsy-turvy. Mine is a *petit-maître*, full of
gallantry and *politesse*, whose only ambition is to arrange
ladies' hair; the other is a mad man who lets his foolish
servant lead him around so that the servant curls *his* hair
with a cooking iron and powders him with a flour sieve.
As for the Spaniard, in the Critic's comedy, he has so

[7] Chiari apparently attempted to extend his attack from Goldoni
himself to the actors in Medebach's company as well.

little to do that aside from his language, there is nothing that distinguishes him. But that poor Italian, vexed and humiliated, treated as an impostor and a counterfeit, really fills me with pity. Alas for Italy if her poets use her thus! What sort of impression will foreigners have, if indeed they ever look beyond their own plays? An Italian ridiculed before three foreigners? A fine show, a fine credit for us! It seems that Italy can only produce counterfeit knights and *Fashionable Adventurers*.[8]

PRUDENZIO: Easy now, Master Polisseno; you will be over your head before you know it. You're criticizing at breakneck speed.

POLISSENO: When you prod a wasp's nest, you shouldn't complain if you're stung. I would be as *innocent of sharp edges as the moon*, or shall we say *as a pot*,[9] if I stood with my hands on my hips and didn't flinch. Men in the know rely on their own, they don't take capital from others. That's how I've acted so far; let others do what they know best.

PRUDENZIO: In other words, are you going to criticize the very play that intends to criticize you?

POLISSENO: This is no time for that. If he prints it and leaves a good margin, I will write out the defects on each page, but the margin would have to be wider than the page itself.

PRUDENZIO: The audience, however, clapped and laughed when they heard that criticism.

---

[8] An allusion to another comedy by Chiari, *L'avventuriere alla moda*, presented in the same season of 1749.

[9] The Italian word *tondo*, literally "round and smooth," carries as well the meaning of "naïve," rather in the manner of the colloquial American use of "square."

POLISSENO: When they laughed they were laughing at themselves, not at me. When the poet had the actor say *blunders*, *blunders*, he was reproving the audience for its applause. Unfortunately, it's all too true that they like to hear condemnations, and there are some who even agree with the slanderers in blaming what they themselves have formerly praised.

PRUDENZIO: So you want to have the *Cunning Widow* presented?

POLISSENO: Why not? For that matter, it should be put on without changing a syllable. If they had made objections before I staged it, I would have believed that it really needed correction; now, by correcting it, I would be cheating the public. Who is criticizing? Try to understand what I am saying without forcing me to speak openly. If I had that much venom in me, I assure you I'd know how to vomit it up in due time. But this good Poet, fearing that I am *infected with venom*, has prepared me a *theriac*, a mixture of stolen plot, copied characters, lines revised and corrected by others, periods made up of various styles mixed together, with an overlay of novelty, which might in effect be called a Masqueraded Mummy.[10]

PRUDENZIO: I don't know what to say; if you want to have your play shown again, go ahead; I won't object, but take care not to insert criticisms or libels.

POLISSENO: I am not one to ridicule people on stage, even if I had good reason to do it. My actors do not dare to speak ill of Poets; they know their duty. Nor would I have ever expected such treatment from those who for so long have been nourished on the milk of my own Muse, and have

[10] Goldoni alludes to Chiari's earlier efforts.

been applauded and highly praised thanks to my poor labors.[11] Master Prudenzio, you are the Reformer of the Theatres, put an end to this wretched abuse while you have time. When playwrights and players speak ill of each other, and use the theatre as a forum for slander, they reach the level of charlatans, and if things go on this way the Theatre will become a pillory. Master Prudenzio, I bid you farewell.

PRUDENZIO: Where are you going in such a hurry?

POLISSENO: Back to my desk, to write my plays.

PRUDENZIO: You haven't been at all depressed by this criticism?

POLISSENO: I am neither so presumptuous as to become boastful, nor so meek as to be disheartened. I do my duty and await my enemy in the arena with my toes dug in. What! Enmity between two Poets who write not for glory but for money? Nonsense, nonsense. Anybody with discrimination will laugh more at us than at our plays. Criticism? Give us our daily bread, not criticism. Whoever wants to live happily and with little effort, let him write for the stage; but let him write like a man, not like a child. *Leaves.*

PRUDENZIO: Master Polisseno has left, and so will I. To tell the truth, I can't blame him for being a bit heated. He deserves credit for having introduced good taste in plays, and now they'd like to drag him down. But they won't, I'm sure they won't. They like him in Venice; in Venice, Justice is done. Criticism? A mere flash in the pan, no more.

---

[11] *The School for Widows* was presented at the theatre of San Samuele in Venice, where Goldoni's earlier plays had appeared.